Ally's Spiritual Journey

A Story of Beating the Odds and Surviving Surgery with Spiritual Healing

Copyright © 2018 by Mary Carol Ross

All rights reserved. No part of this publication may be reproduced by any mechanical, photographic, or electronic process, or in any form of a phonographic recording; nor may be stored in a retrieval system, transmitted, or otherwise be copied for public or private use – other than for "fair use" as brief quotations embodied in articles and reviews without prior written permission.

ISBN 978-0-9998773-2-6 (E-book)
ISBN 978-0-9998773-0-2 (Paperback)
ISBN 978-0-9998773-1-9 (Hardback)

Wild Seas Formatting - (www.WildSeasFormatting.com)
Cover Design by Donna Lingo LingoDesign.net

Published by
In the Light Press
P.O. Box 131705
Carlsbad, CA 92013
publisher@inthelightpress.com

Although the author and publisher have made every effort to ensure that the information in this book was correct at press time, the author and publisher do not assume and hereby disclaim any liability to any party for any loss, damage, or disruption caused by errors or omissions, whether such errors or omissions result from negligence, accident, or any other cause.

This author of this book does not dispense medical advice or prescribe the use of any technique as a form of treatment for physical, emotional, or medical problems without the advice of a physician, either directory or indirectly. The intent of the author is only to offer information of general nature to help you in your quest for emotional, physical and spiritual well-being. In the event you use any of the information in this book for yourself, the author and the publisher assume no responsibility for your actions. This is not intended as a substitute for the medical advice of physicians. The reader should regularly consult a physician in matters relating to his/her health or the health of their pets and particularly with respect to any symptoms that may require diagnosis or medical attention.

Publisher's Cataloging-In-Publication Data

(Prepared by The Donohue Group, Inc.)

Names: Ross, Mary Carol.

Title: Ally's spiritual journey : a story of beating the odds and surviving surgery with spiritual healing / Mary Carol Ross.

Description: Carlsbad, CA : In The Light Press, [2018]

Identifiers:
ISBN 9780999877302 (paperback)
ISBN 9780999877319 (hardcover)
ISBN 9780999877326 (ebook)

Subjects: LCSH: Pets--Diseases--Alternative treatment. | Care of sick animals. | Human-animal relationships. | Spiritual healing.

Classification: LCC SF745.5 .R67 2018 (print) | LCC SF745.5 (ebook) | DDC 636.7/08955--dc23

LCCN 2018901434

1st Edition, February 2018

Printed in the United States of America

This book is dedicated to all animal lovers, big and small;

To Ally and Kody, who have shown me what unconditional love truly is;

To my parents, Magdalene Ross Laqua, Eugene H. Laqua and the late Clyde Benedict "Buckshot" Ross, who always filled our home with many different types of animals to love;

To Robin Willis and Laura Nickolsen, my family members from other lifetimes, for your love and support throughout this process;

To all of those in Spirit, thank you for your support, guidance, energy, and love. Thank you for your downloads of information that were instrumental in creating this book;

and

In gratitude to God with whom all things are possible!

Ally's Spiritual Journey

A Story of Beating the Odds and Surviving Surgery with Spiritual Healing

MARY CAROL ROSS

*Publishing books that bring
light to your life.*

TABLE OF CONTENTS

INTRODUCTION		1
CHAPTER 1.	IN THE BEGINNING	3
CHAPTER 2.	HEALING EMOTIONAL ISSUES	21

    Anxiety Behavior Energies — 26
    Anxiety Causes — 27
    The Anxiety Cure — 28
    Abandonment Behavior Energies — 31
    The Abandonment Causes — 32
    The Abandonment Cure — 34
    Fear Behavior Energies — 36
    Fear Causes — 37
    The Fear Cure — 38
    Victim – Abuse Behavior Energies — 40
    Victim – Abuse Cause — 43
    Victim - Abuse Cure — 43
    Neglect Behavior Energies — 46
    Neglect Causes — 47
    Neglect Cures — 48

CHAPTER 3.	HISTORY OF PHYSICAL HEALTH ISSUES	55
CHAPTER 4.	ALLY'S HOMECOMING AND RECOVERY	93

CHAPTER 5.	THE IMPORTANCE OF THE SPIRITUAL WORLD	105

- Main Joy Guide — 110
- Master Teacher — 111
- Native American Indian — 112
- Medical Doctor — 113
- Business Manager/Doctor — 114

CHAPTER 6.	WHY DID GOD PUT ANIMALS ON THE PLANET?	121

- Animals as Workers — 122
- Animals as Companions — 124
- Animals as Resources — 127
- Animal Roles in the Ecosystem — 128
- The Balancing Act — 132
- The Real Animal Planet — 136

CHAPTER 7.	HELPFUL TIPS FOR BETTER PET RELATIONSHIPS AND A HAPPIER HEALTHIER PET	141

ABOUT THE AUTHOR — 159

ACKNOWLEDGMENTS

Gratitude is always a great starting place for anything in life, including a book. I make it a habit to start every day of my life in a state of gratitude. In keeping with this theme, I begin by expressing appreciation to all of the staff of California Veterinary Specialists (CVS) in Carlsbad, California. Thank you for your expertise and loving energy in your emergency, surgical, and post-op care of Ally.

To all of the wonderful technicians, handlers, and radiologists who spent time with Ally when I could not. It gave me peace of mind that Ally was in the best hands with the love and care all of you diligently provided. Thank you to all of Ally's veterinarians: Dr. Kimberly Doyle, Dr. Glen Grady, Dr. Todd Bowdre, Dr. Tara Hardy, and Dr. Benjamin Polansky. Both Dr. Christian Osmond, DVM, and Dr. Kevin

Bissonnette, DVM, were wonderful surgeons and I thank you for your expert vision and gentle steady hands. Without surgical intervention and post-op care, I don't think Ally would be here today.

To St. Francis and the Divine Order of Spiritual Healing monks and veterinarians: thank you for your loving healing energy for Ally. May you continue to share your blessings with all of those who are in need of your gifts.

Thanks to you for purchasing this book.

INTRODUCTION

Since I was a little girl, I knew I could hear as well as feel the thoughts, words, and emotions of those in the physical and in the spirit worlds. I could communicate with animals, too, and they with me. Not all animals have something to say, but some of them do. It has taken me a number of years to understand and accept my gifts. Within the last decade, I have parlayed these gifts into an unbelievable and amazing ability to heal.

All of my work is God-based. I do not do anything for anyone before asking God to assist me or grant me permission. Prior to every session with my clients, I ask for God's help, guidance, and energy to do what is best for them. I would love to say that it is me who performs healing on my clients. The truth is, it is not me at all. I am just the instrument for God to perform His healing through me.

My intention with this book is to help

other pet parents through difficult times with their babies. I want to share Ally's journey in order to help other pet parents, and so other people will understand the spiritual aspect of animals. I also want to help guide you toward the answers to questions of why animals are here, what happens when they die, and how they are here to help us. I have spent the past thirty years as a student of the metaphysical and the spiritual world; I am excited to share what I have learned with all of you. In doing so, I hope I can plant a seed or open you to something new and exciting. Maybe I can ignite a spark inside of you, or even stoke the burning questions of the unknown.

This book is a true story of one little dog's journey of survival. It's how she beat the odds of sickness and disease to stay here on Earth. It is about the beautiful physical and spiritual healers God sent to assist with her care and recovery.

CHAPTER 1.
IN THE BEGINNING

Ally was born in San Diego, California, on August 13, 2003. Now, she is a 14-year old American Kennel Club–registered American Eskimo canine, which the organization nicknames Eskie. The American Eskimo dog is a breed of companion dog originating in Germany as a member of the Spitz family as a breed first known as German Spitz. In Northern Europe, smaller Spitz were eventually developed into three German Spitz breeds: toy, miniature, and standard. European immigrants brought their Spitz pets with them to the United States, particularly New York, in the early 1900s. All of them descended from larger breeds: German Spitz, the Keeshond, the white Pomeranian, and the Italian Spitz, also known as the Volpino Italiano. Although white was not always a recognized color in the various German Spitz breeds, it has been the generally preferred color in the United States. In a display of patriotism in the era around World War I, Spitz dog owners began referring to their pets as American Eskimo dogs rather than German Spitz.

The American Eskimo was originally bred to guard people and property; it is territorial by nature and a valiant watchdog. The breed in general is not considered aggressive. However, in line with its watchdog history, Eskies are generally quite vocal, barking at any noise, any stranger who comes near, anyone who approaches their owner or their owner's territory. Their characteristics include intelligence, reserve, protectiveness, alertness, and friendliness. Their average life expectancy is twelve to fourteen years.

After World War I, Eskies came to the attention of the American public in a big way as the Eskie dogs became popular entertainers in the circus. While you wouldn't see them jampacked into a clown car, you could see them jumping through rings of fire and doing tricks while on the backs of horses. For instance, in 1917, the Cooper Brothers' Railroad Circus featured the Eskie dogs' agility in their show. In the 1930s, the Barnum and Bailey Circus featured a dog named Stout's Pal Pierre—he was famous for walking a tightrope under the big tent. Due to the appeal of the Eskie dog act, Barnum and Bailey started selling puppies after their shows, thereby growing the popularity and expanse of the breed in the United States. I was told in some of my spiritual classes that in the past, Ally was a little performance dog. To this day she still loves horses.

I like to call Ally a puppy because, as you can tell by her photo on the front cover, she still looks like one, though if you look closely you will see the scar on her chest from her surgery, and her little "boots." Where her legs were shaved for her IVs now looks like she's wearing fur boots. Ally's double fur coat is solid bright white and as soft as cashmere. Her fluffy white tail curls and looks like a constant bouncing cloud floating over her body. Ally has beautiful black saucer eyes with a matching black nose, and a smile with one missing bottom front tooth. On a normal day, she weighs approximately fourteen pounds.

One of Ally's favorite things to do is chase things; her favorite targets are lizards, bugs, butterflies, and birds in the yard. Ally has named her little lizard friends: Lizzy being what Ally thinks is a female lizard, and Albert for the male lizard. The name Albert comes from *Little House on the Prairie* reruns. One of her other favorite things to do is what she calls securing the perimeter, something Ally heard from watching or listening to *Hawaii 50*. She runs outside and walks the perimeter of the back and front yards, mostly looking for her lizard friends and any other unwanted critters. Returning from her outside patrol and announcing to the room, perimeter secure.

When Ally finds something she likes, she does what I call "twirleys." She elegantly dances around in a perfect circle, looking like a little angel with wings in motion. In Ally's younger days, she was extremely agile, loving to jump on all the furniture with ease, no doubt demonstrating her circus heritage breeding. However, she's not always a happy pup as Ally is not particularly fond of other dogs or people coming to the front or back doors. Sometimes she doesn't even like her litter mate, big brother Kody. I think that comes from the way she was treated by her bigger brothers when they were little puppies. To this day, she is not too fond of small children and other dogs.

There were four Eskie puppies in Ally's litter. Their mother was older and, from what I was told, was past her prime for birthing and caring for four puppies. Shortly after the time the litter was born, she rejected them in every way. Since all the puppies in the litter looked like palm sized snowballs with black eyes and noses, the breeder decided to paint the tails of the puppies when they were born in order to tell each puppy apart.

The first puppy of the litter was a slightly larger male and his tail was painted blue. Little Boy Blue was outgoing, confident, and the first to find a home. Second in puppy birth order was another male who had a purple painted tail. Little Boy Purple would later be known as Kody. Ally held birth order position number three; her tail was painted pink. She was considerably smaller than her brothers and the only female of the litter. Due to Ally's size, structure, temperament, and movement (characteristics that allow the breed to perform the function for which it was bred), the breeder was thinking about holding Ally from sale to become a show dog. The last of the litter was Little Boy Yellow. He was the most timid and fearful, and more shy than any of his siblings.

From the very beginning, all of the puppies from the litter displayed the characteristics of being shy, timid, and also full of fear with the exception of Little Boy Blue. A puppy displaying these types of behaviors in their earlier stages of life can be overcome and the puppy will develop into a confident, loving dog. An adult dog can also be healed and rehabilitated into a loving, self-assured dog if they receive the right loving environment and a human with knowledge to assist in their healing. It might not always be an easy path taking on an animal with severe emotional issues, but it will always be rewarding. And yes, dogs—like humans—

can all be rehabilitated and healed. (I have learned in my healing work, fear can quickly escalate into anxiety in both a human and an animal.)

I was not involved in bringing Ally and Kody to their first new home, as it happened before I entered their lives. My sister from another lifetime, Robin, had been the one in search of new fur babies. Robin was still healing from the loss of her other Eskie, Tall-e-ho. Tall-e had been diagnosed with late stage cancer at the age of thirteen, which had gone undetected and undiagnosed for several years. Numerous veterinarians had examined Tall-e, but the cancer was not detected until it prevented her from walking. Due to the amount of pain Tall-e was experiencing, she had to be put down.

To Robin, losing Tall-e was like a single parent losing her only child. It left a huge hole in her heart. You see, several years prior to Tall-e's passing, Robin also lost her mother to breast cancer. Tall-e died on a Sunday in May of 2002, and Robin's father died the Tuesday of the same week. They were big losses for Robin in a very short period of time. The loss of a beloved pet may not seem to be as severe as the loss of a parent. However, a loss of a loved one is a loss. Robin, as we all, needed to go through the grieving process with each loss.

One of her friends was thinking Robin needed some companionship, so as a favor, another of her friends researched Eskies in the area and sought out a reputable local breeder. One Saturday morning in September of 2003, Robin went to view this new litter of puppies, hoping to find a new loved one. While visiting the puppies, Robin sat on the floor and Baby Ally climbed into her lap. As soon as the other puppies came close to Robin, Ally barked at them as if to say, "Go away." Ally was in much need of love and attention. Kody and Little Boy Blue came to check out the new person who had entered their home. Little Boy Yellow, on the other hand, ran away and hid behind a chair. After a short visit, Robin said she wanted some time to reflect; this was a big decision. By this point, it had been a couple of years since Robin had a dog and she needed to truly consider her decision. Did she want one or two puppies? Was she ready to take on this responsibility again?

As Robin left the breeder's home that Saturday morning, she looked back and little purple-tailed Kody had followed her outside the door and was walking toward the gate, as if to say, "I want to go home with you! Don't leave me here." Robin took Kody's following her as a sign that he was the puppy for her.

The next weekend, Robin returned to give Kody a home. Upon her arrival at the breeder's home, Kody greeted Robin immediately, as if he recognized her. Robin was still hoping that Kody was her deceased dog Tall-e, reincarnated.

While continuing her visit, Robin witnessed little pink-tailed Ally and little purple-tailed Kody playing together. The breeder had commented, "They always play together. They're special friends." These two puppies were only two minutes apart in age and they had spent all of their six-week lives together. Ally had a special connection to Kody that she did not have to her other litter mates. Kody was her brother and her friend.

After the loss of her Tall-e, Robin had

hoped that dogs reincarnate and return to their previous owners. When Robin had said goodbye to Tall-e, she had pleaded for Tall-e to find a way back to her. I believe she actually thought Ally was a reincarnation of Tall-e's soul and that swayed her to make the decision to take two puppies home with her that day. (I also don't think Robin had the heart to separate the two little puppies.) Kody and Ally had found a bond and safety with each other, and were then heading to Robin's home.

Once in their new home, Robin named the new family members with an Alaskan theme, since both puppies looked like polar bear cubs. Little pink tail was named Ally Berra, after Mount Alyeska, and little purple-tail was named Kody Bear after the Kodiak bear. Several months after bringing Ally and Kody home, Robin was called upon to commit to extensive work-related travel. She had to depart on Sunday and return on Friday several times a month for more than a year. During this time, Ally and Kody's care was left to pet sitters, and the puppies spent many nights at home by themselves. Luckily they had each other for company.

Most weekends when Robin was home, she took Ally and Kody to play ball or for walks at the doggy park. When it came time to go for their first walk on a leash, Ally wouldn't go. She shied away, ran away, and hid under furniture while Kody was lassoed up in his harness. Ally patiently waited on the steps peering out the window to see if Kody would return. After Kody returned, she wanted to go.

Today, she has to be first for the leash, not to mention the first out the door. Ally still loves to play ball. The only problem is she never wants to give the ball back. Kody isn't into the ball; he prefers to walk off his leash and smell the flowers. They are the epitome of male and female. He is all about food, sleep, and bird chasing. She is all about the attention, affection, and pink sparkle bows.

I came into Ally, Kody, and Robin's life in 2012. At the time, I had made the difficult transition from telecommunications/oil and gas law to becoming a spiritual healer. It was a gradual transition, but a necessary one. Robin had scheduled a healing session with me, so I made it a house call.

Ally and Kody were eight years old at that point, with extensive lung capacity for optimal barking. Ally was, and still is, the boss in the household. Both Kody and Ally seemed to be very hyperactive dogs, with a tremendous amount of anxiety. Ally had been the smallest of her siblings. In comparison, she only weighs fourteen pounds today while Kody weighs thirty.

As a healer, I have come to understand that the early development years of a dog are no different than the early development years of a human. The only difference is that an animal cannot tell you what they experienced. The early experiences help to create and shape our filters on how we show up and view the world.

I can still remember the first time I walked through the front door of Ally and Kody's home to give Robin a soul healing session. She had experienced a rather emotional breakup with a long lost love, and was still grieving over the passing of her parents in addition to her dog, Tall-e. As anyone would be, she was having a hard time moving past all the trauma and her emotional past.

Contrary to Robin's presentation of emotion, both puppies were so excited to meet me. They were barking, jumping, and trying to get through the screened front door to me. I stepped inside and Ally immediately attacked me with kisses, followed by submissive rolling on her back to make sure I would scratch her little pink belly. As long as I was touching her, she stayed right with me. I had an instant connection with Ally. She undoubtedly recognized me on some level. She looked at me with those big dark eyes with happiness and love, and said, "Yes, someone to love me." She took every little bit of attention she could get, soaking it up like a dry sponge plunged into a sink full of warm water.

Kody was excited, and even jumped over Ally to move her out of the way in order to receive some stroking from me. While barking to try to get everyone's attention, he wanted to make sure that he was recognized. However, once acknowledged, he then retreated to Robin.

Later in the afternoon, I remember Ally

hiding underneath the living room ottoman. Robin commented, "She does that all the time. She likes to hide under and behind furniture." You could see her little tail sticking out from the dust ruffle of the ottoman, but Ally was hidden; in her mind, she was safe. Ally was noticeably suffering with a loud honking cough, which reminded me of the noises my grandmother's ducks and geese made.

Kody also had an ailment I noticed. He had a red skin irritation on the lower half of his body, which stood out through his white fur. He looked like he had taken a seat in light red paint. His back legs, front legs, tail, and bottom area were all light red. The irritation was caused by him constantly chewing and scratching his back legs, his tail, and his bottom.

Robin and I met every week for several months for her healing sessions. I made the drive to her home every time. When I would make the turn into Robin's subdivision to her home, I would tell Ally telepathically, "I am coming to see you. Come to the door." Robin would report that if the three of them were in the backyard, Ally would become agitated and want to get into the house. If Ally was inside, she would immediately run to the stairs that allowed her to see into the front yard. Ally had heard me and was looking for me.

Through our session work, Robin and I became good friends. We had similar early childhood experiences and hobbies. There were two instant connections in particular as well as something I would later discover in my past life regression work—Robin and I had been sisters in many other lifetimes. Since we did get along like sisters, a few months later, Robin invited me to live with them. Since I was still transitioning from my corporate legal position to full time spiritual healer, I welcomed the invitation. I became part of their lives in a more permanent way, now one big happy family. I was now a member of the household.

My healing work allows me the luxury to work from home, so I was spending a tremendous amount of time with the puppies. I am not sure which of us enjoyed it more—the puppies or me? By spending most of every day with them, I noticed that both Ally and Kody displayed severe tendencies toward shyness, fear, and anxiety. They never seemed able to settle down and relax. These were the same emotional tendencies Robin displayed. Animals, especially dogs, often take on their owner's emotional issues—or sometimes the animals are attracted to us because they share the same issues. As humans, we attract people and animals who have the same issues as we do. Our animals will mirror our emotional issues back to us.

Every little sound outside the front of the house evoked an immediate, fear based barking frenzy from both puppies—instinctual behavior to alert the pack of coming danger. Ally was always the first to sound the alarm, with Kody chiming in shortly after. The doorbell ringing or the voices on an answering machine instantly activated the barking, which would soon turn into howling. Ally then followed the howling with her goose coughing. The neighbors would comment that this was the house where the psycho puppies live. Trash and gardener days were both filled with tension when it came to the puppies; their barking was so loud it was not even possible to speak on the phone.

Kody "acted out" more than Ally. He was constantly scratching the carpet, rubbing his back and side on the walls, leaving greasy bands along the walls in the house. He had a habit of going into an empty room and barking once before quickly escalating into a continuous howl until one of us would find him and get him to stop by giving him a hug. (I believe this was how Kody expressed that he felt neglected and abandoned, that he needed reassurance that someone was there for him.) At feeding time, Kody would guard both bowls to keep Ally from her bowl. He would knock Ally out of the way to get to any treat first.

It was apparent to me after spending more intense time with the dogs that the emotional fears of both puppies were causing their physical ailments. Ally's need to hide and protect herself and Kody's constant chewing were the result of their emotional issues and anxiety. Being a healer of human physical and emotional issues, I set out to see how I could heal and help these two innocent puppies.

CHAPTER 2.
HEALING EMOTIONAL ISSUES

Animals come into this world in a state of near perfection. Their souls are evolved and whole. Animals do not have any lessons to learn or karmic debts to repay as humans do. Animals show up in our lives ready to be of service, to be loved, and to love their humans. What any animal does bring with them with each incarnation is the emotions from each past life.

Every canine breed has different characteristics that have been bred or inbred into them, such as temperament, size, and color. Canine traits of excessive aggression or even violent behavior were not brought into this lifetime by the dog. They were conditioned by a human to behave in that manner, either by training, breeding, or, I hate to say it, abuse and or neglect. All negativity is brought about by humans. Which means, since humans created it, then humans can also put a stop to it and repair it.

As you have read in the previous chapter, Ally, Kody, and their littermate siblings were all suffering from anxiety, abandonment, and even some fear issues. The abandonment actions are a direct effect of their puppy mother not wanting to have anything to do with them except giving birth. Unfortunately, some of a dog's anxiety and fear issues can also be a direct result of inbreeding practices.

There is another piece to an animal's emotional composition and soul energy that needs to be addressed. Animals do bring some of their issues from their past lives with them into each incarnation. So not every energy issue will be a direct effect of their treatment in this lifetime. As an example, if a dog was neglected and abused in another lifetime, it will bring the memories as well as the resulting energies and exhibit characteristics of being abused to this lifetime even if there was no abuse or neglect suffered by the dog in this lifetime. The cycle will continue until the animal is completely healed from the emotional traumas.

Even if you feel that you may not have the healing abilities with which I have been blessed or the practice to hone the talent you do have, there are still some things you can do to help your fur babies. (I am also available to heal your puppy, too.) When you are trying to heal a puppy, the best medicine you can give is love! Look into the dog's eyes and tell your fur baby that you love him or her. Believe it or not, the puppy will receive the message. Play and spend time with your pet — give them lots of hugs, too! To this day, if I am writing or sitting at my computer and it has been several hours since I gave him any attention, Kody will jump on my leg and ask for a hug.

The other most important tool in your arsenal of healing tricks is to pay close attention to your pet's behaviors. The way they stand, sit, the position of their ears, and tail are all revealing information. A shaking or bouncing tail most probably indicates a happy dog. A tail tucked down or between their legs is fear or anxiety. Ears pinned back signals aggression. Ears perked up means high alert, interest in what is coming.

Animals and humans have many emotional energies as well as issues in common. Humans, however, have a longer list of issues. People come into this world to learn lessons and to settle karmic debts. With animals, their emotional energies are created throughout their short lives, not just in their adolescent years; They too bring into every life time the emotional issues they experienced in their past. If they encounter a human that once abused, neglected, or abandoned them, they will respond to the recognition of the abusive soul by growling or aggressive behavior. The animal will remember. The animal's current behavior can tell you a tremendous amount about their past and how they were treated.

Anxiety, abandonment, victimhood, neglect, and fear emotions are five of the most common issues with dogs, though it is difficult to completely separate one issue from the others because they all fit "into" each other. Sort of like comparing each color of the rainbow, they are all there, creating one beautiful scene. In addition to the rainbow, the colors exist separately.

Please keep in mind that there are different levels of intensity of each emotional issue. Before you begin any healing on your pet, please make sure they are physically fit. A trip to the vet is a good idea to make sure your pet's issues are not caused by disease or physical difficulties. Also remember to reward your pet, as positive reinforcement training is one of the most powerful techniques. Dogs also rely heavily upon predictability and routine; if that routine is disrupted, it can lead to nervousness and fear.

With any emotional pet issue, there are prescription medications that are available to calm your pets, if you choose to go that route. One of my favorite nonprescription go to products for calming an animal in any emotional energy is *Bach's Rescue Remedy by Bach Flower Remedies*. It's available in both cream and drops as a homeopathic remedy created with flower material cut with brandy and water. You can put a few drops on a treat for your pet, in the water bowl for more severe issues, rub cream on trouble spots, or even put on their ears.

Anxiety Behavior Energies

Anxiety is the most common emotional issue for dogs. Anxiety can be present in the other four emotional issues, but not always the cause. Anxious animals frighten easily and find solace in addition to comfort in physically hiding. At the sound of a loud noise or something close to them, they will duck, cover, or run away. The smallest sound will have them running from it. They will appear to be insecure in their actions, displaying a lack of confidence in their behavior and even their existence.

Anxiety can definitely escalate into fear, but not necessarily into either abandonment or victim emotions. Being shy about eating their meals, treats, or even drinking their water are just a few of their skittish behaviors. In addition, they may approach their bowls with extreme caution, look from side to side while they approach, survey other animals, or even monitor their positions toward their food.

An anxiety laden dog will have a

tendency to find a quiet place or even a room to be alone, constantly seeking solitude. It will go to great lengths to find a way to get away from any noise in the home. Anxiety filled dogs are usually not big barkers, yet there are always exceptions to this rule. Veterinarian and grooming visits may elicit an uncontrollable shaking or trembling response. The trembling may continue until the dog perceives the threat to be removed, even shivering when it's 100 degrees outside; that is anxiety that has progressed into a fear response. Sometimes with anxiety issues, when the dog starts trembling they will also suffer from uncontrolled urination.

Anxiety Causes

Anxiety primarily appears in dogs because they were not shown enough love and affection from their canine mothers. Another reason could be there was a large number of dogs in the litter, many other barking dogs nearby, or they were trained with loud correction noises or a human's yelling. Sometimes in potty training dogs, loud noises are used as the correction or to get their attention, as with the sound of pot lids as cymbals. Smaller breed dogs do not respond positively to this type of discipline. (Not sure any dog responds positively to this.)

Another thing that causes anxiety is when dogs have been slightly neglected. By slightly, I mean they had their primary needs met, such as food, water, and potty training, but not a lot of love, attention, or socialization with humans (or other dogs). A good parallel would be children in an overcrowded orphanage. No one was neglected, but there wasn't enough time for a lot of individual attention or love to go around for each puppy. As you previously read, Ally was not neglected to the point of being abused, but her mother was too old to properly love and pay attention to her.

You may also see temporary anxiety behaviors if the anxiety or stress levels in the household rises. Dogs will respond to changes and stress in their homes.

The Anxiety Cure

Exercise is the best tranquilizer for all

animals, especially for dogs. When Ally displayed her anxiety behaviors (i.e. running from a loud noise), I would find her, get down on the floor, and touch or hold her. I would put one arm around her chest and the other around her bottom as to hug her. She would usually lean in to my arms and then lay down in them. I would give her kisses, pet her, and tell her, "You're alright, you are safe," until she stopped shaking. At first it seemed to take thirty minutes before she would stop. With each episode, it became less and less. Today, the shaking has stopped. If there is a loud noise that frightens her, she stands up looking for me. If she cannot find me, she then looks for the nearest exit. Most of the time I don't have to touch her, I just have to say, "You're alright." She quickly returns to her previous place and calmly lies down.

This technique will work for most anxiety riddled dogs. If your dog runs and hides, do your best to find him or her. If you can reach them, pet them. Tell them that they are safe and secure. Don't push or pull them out; if you can coax them out, great. If not, let them come to you. Never force or forcefully move your dog as it will create another level of anxiety. They need to be comforted and reassured they are safe.

Sometimes their favorite treats work in these types of situations as a distraction if they are a food driven pet. When they feel safe and the fear of the threat has gone, they will come find you. If your dog likes to be brushed, gently do that to calm them. There are also alternatives if your presence isn't enough, such as a *Thundershirt*, which is a vest to help with anxiety.

On a normal day, Ally has never liked to be held. She is not a lap puppy, unless something has frightened her, like being at the veterinarian's office, waiting to be checked in at the groomers, or she is physically cold. She does still have some slight shaking or trembling when she is in one of those four situations. I hold her, tell her she is alright, and that she is safe. Each episode gets easier with less trembling. The shivering, however, does not deter her from wanting to go to get her pink sparkle bow.

If the conditions of your pet are severe,

you can see your veterinarian for the appropriate medications.

Abandonment Behavior Energies

Abandonment issues are not as common as anxiety issues. Some dogs who are suffering from abandonment issues may also display traits of separation anxiety. A dog suffering with abandonment issues will usually follow their humans, never allowing their owner out of their sight. When they are left alone, whimpering and whining—even howling—will quickly ensue. Pacing and panting are also abandonment actions. They have a constant need to be touched, spoken to, and have a need for constant company. They need the reassurance that their owner is close at hand.

Abandonment energy also creates the need for a dog to chew or scratch on themselves as well as chewing on convenient objects, most often chewing an area that is easily accessible. On the pet itself, it can be something they can reach with their mouth, such as their limbs and back sides. They will chew until their fur has disappeared, their skin is raw and bleeding. Severe abandonment issues will have your canine friend becoming your shadow, never being more than a foot away from you (including the bathroom and shower).

I have witnessed dogs walk into an empty room looking for their owners, and barking until someone comes to get them or calls for them. This is one of Kody's tricks. Some may also partake in destructive behavior while their owners are gone. This can manifest as tearing up furniture or their owners' belongings, even leaving little potty presents around the room.

The Abandonment Causes

Dogs that have been surrendered by their owners after several years suffer with abandonment issues. They created an attachment to their family and then one day they were left. These types of dogs are always hoping that their family will one day return to claim them. Unfortunately, this surrendering of a pet happens for a number of reasons: financial, wrong breed for the family, and even death of the owner. I don't think the abandonment of a dog is as severe as it is to a child, but make no mistake, it is hard on the animal. Usually the owner does not explain to the dog that they have to go away; they just leave the pet.

Another incident causing stress would be to a new puppy in a new home. Stress is created when the owner leaves it alone for long periods of time before the puppy is acclimated to its new surroundings. The third type of stress akin to abandonment would be having a dog without ever interacting with it, basically emotionally checking out of the dog-to-human relationship.

You may also see a temporary display of abandonment traits if you were gone and left your dog in the hands of a pet sitter. In addition, dogs that were deprived of their mothers as young animals, or weaned too early, will also fall into this category. I believe Ally falls into this category. She was suffering from some of these abandonment issues in the past from both her puppy mother and Robin.

The Abandonment Cure

In the beginning, it is not a good idea to leave a dog suffering from these issues alone for longer than an hour at a time. They need the reassurance that you will be returning to them. When you leave, give them a treat. This way they will see your departure as a good thing. Every day, you can build up the time you are away.

An alternative to a treat for younger dogs is lush bedding. Puppies will respond well to their own bedding or blankets. They benefit from something that belongs to them, and them alone. As you are working up to the longer away times, it is a good idea to put in their bed or crates something that you have used, like a worn piece of clothing or used bath towel. For instance, you can wear a t-shirt for a day and then put it in their home, crate, or bed. (A used pillow case will also work well.) That way they know your body scent and feel you are near. Dogs explore the world with their noses. It will also bring a sense of calmness to the animal in your absence.

Another way to distract the dog is to leave

on a television or radio to help with the silence. Most importantly, don't forget the tranquilizer, i.e. exercise. It will also help you form a bond with your new fur baby.

If you are truly concerned about your pet being alone, you might want to consider bringing another dog into your family. At most times, a companion dog will be beneficial with abandonment and separation anxiety ridden dogs. Neither dog will feel alone if there is another dog present.

The most important piece to curing your dog's abandonment issues to give them several big hugs a day. A hug that brings the dog's ears to your heart. Pets need to hear your heart beat. There is something extremely comforting to an animal when he or she can hear your heart beat. It probably goes back to their own mothers, and the comfort felt while hearing the beat of her heart when they were young. The animal will let you know when they have had enough hugging when your pet feels it's time to pull away.

Fear Behavior Energies

Fear is a more complex emotional issue than the other two have been. Dogs that are suffering with fear issues may also have anxiety and abandonment issues. The biggest difference between fear and the previous two is usually the barking, the need to hide.

Dogs that are fearful will bark at every turn and at everything. It can start with the one bark and quickly escalate into the rapid instinctual response of "alerting the herd" constant barking, continuing to the point of showing their teeth with their ears pinned back in full attack mode.

Other fear traits can be cowering, trembling, drooling, destructive behavior, and in some cases aggression. If a dog's anxiety and abandonment issues have been left untreated, it can definitely evolve into fear. Depending upon the severity of the fear, it can also cause a dog to lose control of its bladder or bowels. Also, dogs with fear issues will not want to try new things. They shy away from new toys, furniture, and people.

Fear Causes

Possibly the hardest emotional issue to diagnose and treat is idiopathic fear, that is fear with an unknown cause or triggers. Most dogs suffering from idiopathic fear have been physically and emotionally abused. One of the most common causes of fear is fireworks or other loud noises, such as: vacuum cleaners, air compressors, gun shots, and thunder.

When dogs are not properly socialized at a young age, other dogs and strangers may also create a fear response. Sometimes people think they are desensitizing an animal, but train with loud noises, and that can elicit a fear response to those noises. Additionally, some dogs suffer from fear of men, riding in vehicles, and stairs just to name a few sources of fear.

Other types of fear are conditioned into the dog. For instance, if a dog has been abused by a man, it will have a fear response to most men. A gun shot may be hurtful to the animal's ears besides the fear of the loud sound. Basically, if a dog has not been exposed to an activity, they will have a fear of it. It boils down to the fear of the unknown. (Humans also have this fear issue in a major way.)

The Fear Cure

For most, general fear creates a response because it is the fear of the unknown. Desensitization is the key to healing any fear in an animal. Take your time to slowly introduce your pet to one of its fears. Slowly introduce the new activity, perhaps riding in a car. Take short rides with lots of treats. Make it as pleasant an experience as you can for your dog. Every other day increase the distance.

One of my favorite tricks is to load the dog in the car, then reward him with treats, with the end of the short ride be to the doggy park. Take him out, then let him run and play ball. With this activity, the dog will associate the vehicle ride with a fun activity. With most dogs, the only trip they ever take in a vehicle is to the vet's office. No wonder they don't want to ride in a car. Vehicle rides need to be associated with more pleasurable outings.

With a fear of the stairs, that's an easier

one. Place treats on every other step and reward your pet with love and treats when they reach the top. Sometimes it helps if you go first, to show them how it's done and that it is a safe activity.

With a fear of men, you would have to first heal the victim issues with the animal. (We will cover that in the next section.) If it is possible, when your dog comes in contact with a man, have them bring treats with them. The idea here is to establish a pleasurable response from the dog while interacting with a man. Don't force the connection, but allow the pet to come around to the male human without loud noises or sudden movements. Slow, steady, and frequent is the key to overcoming this type of fear.

Fireworks and thunder are other easier ones to overcome. Keep your pet as far away from the fireworks as possible. If you live nearby a loud fireworks display, please do not leave your dog alone in the dark while you go and enjoy the fireworks. Make sure your pet is close to you and if not contained inside the house, make sure they are on a leash. Loud sounds can cause a dog to run. I have also seen a dog rip though a screen window to get away from lightning. You want to make sure you prevent that with a temporary solution, like *Bach Flower Remedies*, but you still need to resolve the fear issue.

The fear of strangers may be the most difficult to overcome. The best way is to slowly introduce your dog to many new people. Before any outing, make sure your dog has been fed as well as exercised. Exercised dogs are more calm and less anxious. Slowly begin to socialize them with new neighbors or friends. Move gradually into more public type of places. Pay close attention for signs of aggression. If any aggression signs appear, instantly touch your dog and remind them they are safe. The more socializing you do with your dog, the easier its fear of people is to overcome. Make sure, as you are socializing your pet, that you diligently watch your pet's body language. You do not want to inflict stress.

Victim – Abuse Behavior Energies

Victim energies are the most difficult

issues to discuss. I don't know why anyone would abuse any animal, much less a dog. Unfortunately, it does happen in our society. Dogs that have been abused display anxiety, fear, and abandonment issues. There may also be physical signs of trauma. Dogs with victim issues will flinch or pull away when a human attempts to pet or touch them. They normally will shy away from humans at all costs, even going so far as to hide in their crates or a convenient corner.

Most abused dogs will display tails down between their legs and hanging their head. They also can take the opposite role to a perceived threat by clinging to their human, even climbing into their laps as a defense mechanism in order to defuse the situation. Not all dogs adopt this behavior; it depends upon the temperament of the dog.

In extreme cases of fear, the trust between the dog and human has been broken and lost. During contact with humans, a dog who may have been abused will urinate or have instant bowel movements. Training an abused dog can be more difficult because the dog does not trust humans. It has been conditioned to fear them. It will become startled or fearful when you raise your voice, if there is a loud noise, or someone makes a sudden move. Some abused dogs may become aggressive as they will try to defend themselves when they identify a possible threat. They may attack a human or other animals. Different objects (bats or even tennis rackets as examples) as well as a word or a tone of voice used by the former owner may be triggers.

The signs will be somewhat evident. A dog who has been abused by kicking will avoid a person's feet. If any person comes close to the animal with his or her feet, the dog will begin to cower and run away. The abused dog has been conditioned to fear all humans. Fear manifests because pain caused by a human has been inflicted upon the dog either emotionally, physically, or both. Yelling at a dog for a continuous amount of time is also considered abuse. Dogs do respond to our voices and the tones of our voices, the same way a child would. Not all dogs are going to understand everything that is being said to them, but the majority of them will understand every word.

Victim – Abuse Cause

Sometimes I think people take on animals to fill a void in their lives or they chose to become pet owners for the wrong reasons. Animals should be brought into a human's stable life to enhance their lives, not to fix something. When a new animal is brought into a household that may be fragile or volatile, the pet can bring added stress to the situation. The dog becomes the escape for someone else's anger. Something inside of the human is needing a power trip to make themselves feel better.

The other problem would be that the offender is being abused themselves, so they feel it is normal. I wish I could tell you that I could get into the head of people who are animal abusers. If I could, maybe I could help them change their behavior and save a pet, (a child) or a thousand.

Victim - Abuse Cure

There are two vital points to remember if you suspect your dog has been a victim of abuse. One is please do not expect change in your pet overnight. Secondly, you should not expect a complete turnaround in the animal's trust level or behavior. There may always be some sort of small triggers of the memory of the abuse.

It takes time to help an abused dog learn to be less fearful and develop trust in humans again. With knowledge, hard work, and commitment, a previously abused pet can be transformed into a much loved member of your family.

To do this, you need to create a safe and secure world for your pet. Make your pet feel loved and needed. Communicate with him or her with a soft loving tone of voice. Look into his or her eyes while you speak. Do not under any circumstances force anything on the abused pet or any other type of pet. Give them all the space and time they need to adapt to their new family.

Let the pet adapt at their own pace. Make sure he or she has a safe place if the animal is needing solitude. Do your best to protect him or her from whatever brings them fear. Create opportunities for your pet to be successful and build confidence, even as simple as going potty outside. Praise him or her with words, affection, and treats for the smallest accomplishments. Exercise is recommended, though extra care should be given if there are leash and collar fears present. If so, find a safe fenced yard or dog park to slowly introduce the collar and leash.

A Sound Beginning is a program available to assist with abused animals. It was lovingly and expertly designed to help rescue dogs and adoptive parents learn to communicate effectively with each other, creating trust and an unbreakable bond. Depending on the triggers for your dog, you may need to invest in this type of program.

The experts will tell you rehabilitating an abused dog presents a significant challenge, because the animal has been exposed to negative things he or she can't unlearn despite your best efforts. I agree rehabilitating does pose extreme challenges, but I don't agree that the animal cannot unlearn or be completely healed from their past. They can! Every type, breed, and trauma of any dog can be retrained.

Neglect Behavior Energies

Neglect is the easiest to determine. Neglect behaviors will have some similar behaviors to abuse and victim behaviors. Dogs that are suffering from neglect will display both physical and emotional neglect. Unfortunately, many dog owners think chaining their dog is acceptable. Tossing some food and water into bowls is enough. Let me say it is not acceptable or enough!

One of the major differences with neglect energies is the physical signs. Dogs that have been neglected will be emaciated or alternatively obese. They either have had the wrong types of food, such as human food, or no food at all. Dehydration is also a big problem with neglected animals. There may be cuts, bruises from heavy chains or collars around their necks, and even burns from unsafe living conditions. There will be a lack of grooming, dirty matted fur, even bald spots, with long, broken, and jagged nails. Parasite infestations may also be present. Dogs become aggressive toward other dogs or their humans when food is present is also a sign of neglect. They will also shy away from humans, or even growl when being approached.

Neglect Causes

I would like to think that no one ever acquires, or purposely brings, an animal home to abuse or to neglect it. My answer to these causes is uneducated owners. Dog owners often do not know how to correctly care for their pets or particular breed of dog. Some people think a dog is a dog. No, there are different types of dogs with many different needs. Maybe the family's financial or housing circumstances changed. Or the human has become ill and has not been able to properly care for their pet. I believe most human companions are not properly prepared for the commitment in the proper care of a dog.

When I was growing up, we adopted many neglected and abandoned animals. We lived in the country off a county road. At night with a new moon it was dark, very dark, and the primary place for people from surrounding counties to dump their unwanted dogs, cats, puppies, and kittens. I am assuming they opened their automobile doors and literally threw their pets out of it. From some of the injuries these abandoned dogs were suffering, the human did not even stop the car before throwing the animal. These little animal souls always found their way to our door for food, love, and attention.

Neglect Cures

The first and most obvious one would be to feed them, give them water, and get them to the veterinarian's office as soon as possible. Assess their physical issues. Do the best you can to take care of their physical needs. Sometimes a neglected dog will not allow a human close to them. Approach with caution. If they will not allow touching or petting, just be present, talk to them in a calm and loving manner. With abused animals, their trust with humans has been broken. Time, structure, and consistency is what is needed to rebuild the trust.

Depending upon the severity of the neglect, you might have to work with all of the other four conditions (anxiety, abandonment, fear, abuse) as the layers of issues began to surface. The current issue the dog is displaying is what gets the most attention.

If you are one of those special people who has adopted a neglected animal, I send you many blessings. That is not an easy road to walk. However, if you have the tenacity and commitment to help the animal heal, you will have a loyal friend for life.

Now, I understand most folks may not be able to speak to animals or hear them in the way I am able. However, pay attention because your dog is trying to communicate with you through their actions and inactions — you will be able to tell. Your dog needs your love and attention. Speak to all of your animals as if they can understand you, as most of them can! Dogs are not meant to simply be fed and then left alone. They are very social creatures. They need to spend time with their owners. They are like perpetual two year old children. Always find time to spend some quiet time each day with your new (or familiar) pet.

If you want to dig deeper into your dog's emotional issues, outside of those listed above, one of the best places to look is in the mirror. The other good starting point is their past, to see what they have been through. This also applies to other animals, like horses and cats. In my experience, though, dogs are more blatant and demonstrative with their issues than cats.

As owners, we can easily transfer our emotional issues to our pets. An animal will pick up on the energy in the room or the emotion of its owners. When you hear the comment that dogs can feel your fear, it is a true statement. I firmly believe that as a human, our thoughts are powerful. What we believe, we become. Our unresolved issues (like resentment, anger, or fear) can cause issues, ailments, and diseases within our physical bodies. If you heal or release the trapped emotions, then you are, in fact, healing the physical body. The same principle applies to animals.

Ally and Kody both took on Robin's fear of being abandoned. Ally took on Robin's feelings of being unsafe and needing protection. Kody took on her constant anxiety. If we take a look at Ally and Kody's past, we can see they were left alone for long periods of time, which could have also created negative emotions such as being abandoned. In this case, Ally and Kody had their own abandonment, fear, and anxiety issues in addition to the ones taken from Robin.

One of my favorite examples of "like attracts like" with respect to emotion is in the commercial for Pedigree dog food. The story opens with a dog being rescued from starvation and abandonment. After being cleaned up and fed, it is put up for adoption in a shelter. A veteran goes to the pound looking for a dog. The veteran has a prosthetic leg, though internal wounds are not visible to the public. He kneels down next to a dog run, points to the cute dog, and asks the woman assisting him, "What about this guy?" Her comment was, "He has been through a lot."

We don't know the backstory of the dog other than the rescue and bath. But the advertisement does insinuate that the veteran chose a dog that has also been through many negative experiences. The commercial ends with "Dogs bring out the good in us, and Pedigree brings out the good in them." I do believe dogs and animals in general bring out the good in us. They also amplify what we have happening in our lives. We don't know the complete history of either the veteran or the dog, but we can see signals about how both are feeling as a result of their history.

Animals help us heal. How many therapy dogs and emotional support dogs are doing that very thing? They bring our own issues to light by their behavior. If we pay attention, we can learn a great deal from our furry little pals. With Ally and Kody, I was determined to help them by helping their owner first.

I started the healing process with Robin, helping her to resolve her own fears and anxiety. After Robin's healing was in motion, I turned my attention to Ally and Kody. I began my God healing work with Ally, similar to what I used on Robin and all of my clients. We began by releasing and transforming her fear of being abandoned, then installed confidence and the feeling of I am safe in her energy field. In addition, I made sure Ally was supported on a physical level.

It is important to support both animals and people with internal healing on a spiritual level as well as the support they need on a physical level for a full recovery.

Within a month of my healing and the physical practices, Ally was no longer hiding under the furniture and Kody didn't chew on himself. Ally turned her hiding into rolls on her back and wiggles in happiness. The puppies' healing took longer than usual due to the high level of fear and anxiety in the household at the time. Releasing the emotion in a dog or a human is the easy part. Once the emotion is gone, the body can heal itself. Sometimes, the physical body can take up to three months to completely heal itself, depending upon the severity of the injury.

I am happy to report that today, Ally and Kody are completely different puppies. They are calm, relaxed, and happy dogs. Every once in a while, they bark a little when a stranger comes to the door, but nothing like their previous behavior. I have to add that Robin is also a completely different person today! She is more confident, happy, and no longer has any self-destructive habits.

CHAPTER 3. HISTORY OF PHYSICAL HEALTH ISSUES

As puppies, neither Ally nor Kody suffered from any major health issues. Of course, like any puppies in new surroundings they had the occasional cough, throwing up if their food did not agree with them, or those days after their vaccinations where they weren't themselves.

Once a year, a quick trip to the vet and maybe a round of antibiotics or a shot would have them back to their bouncy selves very quickly. The worst I had seen was when one of the groomers had gotten too close to Ally's skin with the shears. She had two very large orange sized spots of red bloody skin in both of her front armpits. Needless to say, they no longer go to that chain of pet stores for grooming. Outside of that, there was nothing that was truly debilitating.

However, since I have met Ally, over the past five years, Ally had been to the veterinarian's office numerous times with throat or coughing issues. The attending vet would usually prescribe antibiotics or steroids and the symptoms would resolve. The American Eskimo breed is predisposed to have a collapsed trachea (which has a symptom of coughing) and hip dysplasia, so I watched in particular for those problems.

One winter evening, when I picked up Ally to hold her (as when it's cold she likes to be held and have her belly rubbed) she squealed in pain. We went to the vet. The exam determined Ally was suffering with neck pain. She was given many rounds of steroids, plus medications for pain and anxiety. The x-rays found that Ally did not have any cartilage or cushion between her vertebrae in her upper spine. There wasn't a fix for this particular issue. The recommend-dation was to keep her comfortable and out of pain with medications, restrict her activity, and keep her calm.

This was to be the first of three bouts of neck spinal issues for Ally. With each episode

Ally would require anti-inflammatory medication, oral and injectable steroids, and anti-anxiety and pain medications. It was a difficult time with her during these episodes; if she would turn her neck a certain way, she would squeal in pain. The medications made her sleepy, gave her an unquenchable thirst, and the appetite of a horse. She would wake up every three hours and need to go outside to potty. Keeping Ally calm through any, let alone all of these things, would prove to be a bigger issue than her taking the pain meds.

The third bout was the most severe. Ally was in tremendous physical pain with constant squealing. It got to the point that she was in so much pain I could tell she was using astral travel, where she was going in and out of her body to escape the pain and to decide whether to remain on Earth or make the transition to the other side. Astral travel occurs any time a soul exits from its current physical body and projects itself to another place while remaining attached to its physical body. The other places can be to visit someone in the physical or in the spiritual world. This technique or gift is not limited to animals—humans can do it, too.

After her shots of pain meds and steroids from the vet, she would remain motionless for hours, slipping in and out of consciousness. I decided that if it was best for Ally to make the transition, then that is what needed to happen. I didn't want to lose her. I didn't want to be without this precious little puppy I had grown to love, but it wasn't about me. I sat down next to Ally in her little bed, with my hand on her back, stroking her and petting her face. I closed my eyes and said to her…

> *Ally, if this is too much for you, if you're in too much pain and don't want to be here any longer, you have my permission to go to the Light on the other side. I don't want you to leave, but I understand if you are ready to go. My decision is your decision. I will love and support you no matter what your decision. You will always be with me in your heart. I love you, baby girl.*

I like to call this prayer my Blessing of

Freedom. That was the first of many nights that I have recited this Blessing of Freedom to Ally. At my encouragement, Robin had a similar conversation with Ally. Within several hours, she was conscious, active, and hungry.

This prayer also works on humans. Sometimes, when we are in the midst of losing a loved one, our tendency is to hang on to them for ourselves. We may not consider what is best for them, but only consider what we want. (If you are going to use my Blessing of Freedom, please remember to speak from your heart and soul to your loved one's heart and soul.)

After Ally recovered, she would tell us that St. Francis, a Master Teacher, came to visit her while she was in and out of consciousness. She also told us that when she was in a lot of pain, she would go to the other side (Heaven) and play with the Angel puppies in spirit. They would run on the green grass in a beautiful field with other Angel puppies. It would soon become her happy place to escape.

Ally continued to be somewhat fragile.

Some days were better than others. Some days she would be stronger with more energy; others she would be more lethargic and sleep for the majority of the day. She remained on pain medications when needed. Every time she expended more energy than a normal day or took part in greater activity such as a long walk or playing ball, the next few days were what we called "exhaustion days." It would take her several days to recover from an exercise day. Even going to the groomers was followed by several exhaustion days. Kody had experienced the same type of exhaustion days, but Ally's seemed more severe and longer lasting.

Ally now walked more slowly. She climbed the stairs either very deliberately or not at all. There were days when she would sit at the bottom of the stairs and ask to be carried. The vet continued saying it was because of her neck issues. On the days when Ally would not navigate the stairs, she was given pain medications (Gabapentin and Trazodone), which seemed to get her back to normal. Sometimes too much so! The Gabapentin seemed to make her more energy to a hyper state, and then anxiety would begin. The Trazodone would calm her down.

Since I primarily work from home, I have the luxury of having both dogs with me for most of the day. If I am on the phone with a client, Ally lies to my left side and Kody lies on my right. When I go into meditation to do my spiritual healing work, they are normally sitting within inches of me. They lie there silently, quietly absorbing the beautiful energy of God as I work to heal my human clients. In the quietness of my mediation, I connect with God to see what is best for my clientele. My work, in simple terms, is with His help, I release negative emotions and replace them with positive ones. By releasing the negative emotion (i.e. anger) and replacing it with love, it allows the physical body to heal itself back to the normal state of being healthy.

After Ally's last episode of neck pain, the vet said there wasn't much he could do for her. I decided it was time for God to take over this situation and He could use me as His catalyst to direct specific help for her. I spent some time doing God energy healing to replace the cartilage back into her vertebrae.

This was something new for me. I had never tried to replace body parts in a person, much less a dog. So, I did what I do with all of my human clients—I asked God for guidance, pictured the problem, and performed what I was being told. In Ally's case, I pictured her neck in perfect working condition. From that day forward, Ally did not require as many pain meds. She seemed to be improving more and more each day.

It was a Sunday afternoon in November 2016. I was watching a Dallas Cowboys football game, and I looked down momentarily at Ally lying in her little bed in front of the television. (Ally and I always watch the games together.) I noticed she was shaking uncontrollably. Her regular vet was closed on Sundays, so Robin searched for a vet that was open and found the California Veterinary Specialists of Carlsbad (CVS). I scooped Ally up into my arms and we went to the emergency vet.

By the time we made it there, Ally had stopped shaking and she was acting like her little, bouncy self again. We were given more pain meds for what they thought was due to her neck and sent us home. As the months passed, Ally seemed to be dealing with a low level of constant pain. She would say that she hurt, but she was unable to tell me what hurt or where. I understand not everyone can hear what animals are trying to say, but sometimes simply watching their actions or even their inactions is enough. Ally began to slow down more in her activities.

One Friday morning in April 2017, I woke up to see blood spots with mucus on the carpet. Having two dogs in the house, it was hard to determine which dog had the problem. Neither dog was displaying any conditions or symptoms, so I decided to take the wait and see approach. My intuition told me it was Ally. Indeed, on Saturday morning, she started saying she hurt and that she needed to go to the vet. Ally hates going to the vet, and usually has to be bribed with a sparkly gold bow to even to go to the groomers. So, for Ally to ask to go to the vet, I knew she must be in pain.

Since it was Saturday, we took Ally back to Carlsbad Veterinary Clinic. Dr. Grady examined her, took a set of x-rays, and determined her airway was constricted. While Dr. Grady was reviewing Ally's x-rays, he commented that he would never know by looking at the images that Ally was almost fourteen years old. He said she could easily live another five to ten years. He continued to examine her test results to determine what was the cause of her discomfort on this visit.

What I found interesting when this vet discussed the imaging results, was that there was no mention of the neck issue that had been diagnosed several years earlier. Had my God-energy healing work, performed on Ally years ago, truly corrected the missing cartilage in her neck? Well, there it was in black and white. No issue remaining. As I sat there, I thought, Hmm…Ally hasn't been complaining about her neck for over a year. Robin and I were able to pick her up without any squealing or whining. Could it be this has really been working? I think Ally would tell you all that yes, it was!

The consensus on that visit was to take a conservative approach—to give her some medication and watch her. Ally was not displaying any other symptoms. In fact, she was trying to do her best to escape from the examination room. When we got home, Ally acted like her normal self.

By the following Wednesday morning, I noticed Ally was moving more slowly and sleeping more. In the past when she was taking medications, they would affect her in the same way. When Ally or Kody are not feeling up to par, they gravitate to my room, more than usual, which is full of crystals. The crystal energy seems to not only heal them, but also keeps them calm. That is just what she started doing again.

The next day, she was moving even more slowly and refused to climb the stairs. She would take a step or two, then sit down to rest and repeat. This was not normal behavior. I scooped her up and carried her upstairs to her little bed in my office. I went about my work as usual, and every ten minutes I reached down and petted her. About an hour into our morning, Ally started shaking uncontrollably, her little tongue hanging to one side outside of her mouth. I have to admit, it frightened me! I once again scooped Ally from her little pink bed and put her in the front seat of my car.

As I drove those two miles back to the emergency vet's office, I noticed Ally was drifting in and out of consciousness. Her little black saucer eyes looked at me and she said, "What is happening to me? Mary Carol, don't let me die." I tried my best to keep one hand on her and one hand on the wheel. I asked God and my guides to please get us there safely. Those two miles seemed to take forever!

When I pulled into the parking lot, Ally was still unresponsive, still trembling with her tongue hanging out of her mouth. I carried her from my car and laid her on the check-in desk of the clinic. The receptionist called for a tech to the front STAT. Two vet technicians ran out and lifted Ally to take her to the back. As the technician lifted her, Ally screeched in pain. I sat waiting in the lobby for several hours. Several other dogs came and went, some happy, some not so happy. In between, I could hear Ally squealing with agony. I closed my eyes and sent her as much healing energy as I could conjure during such a stressful time.

Those several hours felt like an eternity. Eventually, I was taken to an examination room, and Dr. Kimberly Boyle appeared, though was immediately called away for another emergency. Upon her return, Dr. Boyle told me that Ally seemed to be in a lot of pain when her lower back was being manipulated, but they couldn't be sure so more testing was needed. They needed to keep Ally in their hospital, as she was still in a tremendous amount of pain. An MRI was ordered, and I was sent home.

When I got into my car to drive home, I sat there for a moment to say my favorite protection prayer for Ally. I call it my God's Bubble Blessing.

> *Dear God, please put and keep this puppy in Your wonderful loving, healing white Light. Heal her from all of her ailments. Keep her protected, calm, and safe. Remove any and all anxiety she is experiencing and replace it with joy and happiness. I leave her, dear God, in Your loving hands.*

This is a blessing I have used on all animals I see that are frightened or scared. When I have to leave Ally and Kody, I also use this blessing. When I return, I usually find them sound asleep on the floor. I also perform this blessing every night for both Kody and Ally.

This Bubble Blessing and Protection Prayer is also good for humans!

I left the vet's office and went home to Kody, who was not happy that he had been left alone. Kody and Ally had never been apart for longer than a few hours.

Several hours passed before the vet called with the result of Ally's MRI. The image showed a herniated disc in her lower lumbar L1 and L2 region. By then, it was late afternoon on Thursday, so surgery was not scheduled until the next day. I asked Dr. Boyle if Ally was still in a lot of pain. She said Ally had been given shots to ease her discomfort, and she was now resting comfortably. Ally needed to remain with them overnight for constant monitoring.

When I went to bed, I could not wrap my head around the fact that Ally needed back surgery. Could it really be causing her so much pain? Something didn't feel right to me. And did Ally really want to undergo this type of surgery? Would it benefit her? Or were Robin and I being selfish still wanting her to stay with us? Even for a human, back surgery is no easy task. It's a long painful process that involves months of slow recovery. For an animal, it would be much worse.

Thankfully, while Ally was sedated, I could still sense her little soul. She left her body and came and visited us at home. I remember, right before I went to bed, I sat down and visualized Ally sitting in front of me. I told her once again,

Ally, I love you very much. You're in the hospital with the vet because you have an injury to your back. The vet wants to put you under and operate on you to fix your back. After the surgery, you'll have to be confined and move slowly, but you can come home. It might hurt a bit, but the vet will do their best to keep the pain away. I don't want you to leave or die; however, if this is too much for you and you don't want to have the surgery,

I understand. You can transition to the other side and become a real Angel puppy in Heaven for St. Francis. The choice is up to you. I will love you no matter what you decide. You will always be with me and in my heart.

On Friday morning, surgeon Dr. Christian Osmond called to say he would be the one performing the surgery on Ally. He also said the radiologist had reviewed the MRI imaging and had seen some fluid around Ally's left lung. This would have to be addressed before back surgery could be performed. The next step involved aspirating some fluid from around her lungs that he said indicated some type of infection, possibly from a foreign material. Next, they would perform a CT scan to more fully understand the source of the lung fluid. I waited to hear what they found.

Dr. Osmond called after the CT scan, while Ally was still under anesthesia. He indicated there was indeed a foreign substance in her left lung, as he had suspected. It would need to be surgically removed. There was pus and fluid in her chest cavity, which also needed to be cleared. This was also likely a source of her cough when she became overly excited, and a light turned on. This made more sense to me. I felt like this was indeed the source of Ally's pain, not her back.

The technical medical term is pyothorax, which is an infection in the chest cavity usually caused by bacteria that enters through the lungs or esophagus. This is a fairly common form of respiratory distress in both dogs and cats. It's quite a serious disorder, and it can be fatal if not treated promptly and aggressively. Pyothorax is an accumulation of pus in the chest cavity between the lungs and the chest wall, caused by an infection. Pus in the chest cavity does not form abscesses like pus in other parts of the body. Instead, it creates a wall of tissue around itself to slow down the spread of bacteria, and pus in the chest forms into sacs that cling to the pleura, the lining around the lungs. This results in scarring and severely impaired lung function.

Dr. Osmond mentioned that, in fact, may be the primary cause of Ally's pain. He said it was a common issue with Dobermans and retriever breeds. When they retrieve a ball or game, sometimes they aspirate plumes or needle-like leaves into their lungs. The debris becomes lodged, compromising their breathing as well as lung capacity. Dr. Osmond suggested this may have happened to Ally. The last time Ally had truly played ball was several years ago. Could this foreign material have been in her lungs all of this time?

Ally originally went into the ER on this visit shaking and unresponsive. Then it escalated to a herniated disc; now it appeared to be an issue with her left lung requiring surgery. All of this happened within thirty-six hours. Meanwhile, Ally had not had anything to eat since Wednesday evening, in addition to being away from home and her loved ones.

Dr. Osmond called me on Friday afternoon after the completion of Ally's surgery. He said her surgery went well, but she would have a long recovery. He had to remove one of the lobes of her left lung in order to fully remove the foreign matter, which had then been sent off for analysis. From what Dr. Osmond could see when performing the surgery, Ally's other lobes looked good. The only one compromised was the one that had been removed. He said normal lung tissue looks somewhat like a sponge; however, the removed left lung lobe looked like liver tissue, thick and dense. The foreign matter had attached itself to the inside of Ally's lung and created a hardened cocoon like substance.

During the early days of her recovery, she remained on a heart monitor and a breathing tube to make sure her lungs exchanged air properly after surgery. There was a drainage tube and three IV ports hooked up to her little legs. Due to the nature of the surgery, a twelve-inch incision had been made down Ally's chest, and her ribcage spread open to access her lungs. Her hair had been shaved completely from her chest and belly then up her back for proper placement of a heart monitor. Through her IVs, Ally was given several different types of antibiotics as well as fentanyl for pain.

I really wanted to see Ally because it had

been several days. Dr. Osmond suggested waiting a day or two after surgery before visiting. Ally was still very much out of it and needed to rest. The last thing I wanted to do was disrupt her recovery, so I agreed. Ally had been placed in an oxygen crate, a specialized piece of equipment where oxygen and medication for breathing treatments can be pumped into the closed area to assist in her recovery, so I knew they were doing everything possible for her.

Saturday morning, I woke up to Ally's little soul on my bed — she had astral traveled to me and I felt her presence. I moved the covers and she said to me, "Mary Carol, whatcha you doing?" Kody told me later that morning that Ally had also visited him and Robin in Robin's room. I think Ally was escaping her body to deal with the pain better. I asked her if she wanted us to come and visit and she said, "No, I will come and visit you."

I called the vet several times per day to check on her. I always got the same response: she was resting comfortably. When I asked if she was going to make it, the answer was always the same. "I don't know for sure; she has been through a lot." Ally was also not eating. The vet technicians recommended I bring them her food, on the chance that she would eat that. She was still in the oxygen crate and her drainage tube was still being productive, so it would remain. I sent her healing light and my God's Bubble Blessing and Protection Prayer during meditation each night.

By Sunday, they still couldn't get her to eat. While I was meditating and performing my healing energy work on human clients, I did some more God energy healing work on Ally at the same time. She showed up in my meditation as a happy, carefree puppy. She was running and playing ball in a beautiful green field with other puppies in spirit. Some of my joy guides and St. Francis were playing with her. She may not have been able to physically play ball at the time, but at least her soul was able to play while astral traveling.

On Sunday morning during my meditation and prayer, I learned that St. Francis was helping Ally to heal. In the spiritual world or the spiritual side of life, or Heaven if you will, there is an entire staff of Master Teachers, Spiritual Guides, Angels, Indians, and many other helpers for humans as well as animals. That day, I learned there is also a Divine Order of spiritual monks that are specifically sent to Earth to help humans and animals heal. Within this particular Divine Order, there are monks designated specifically for animals.

Growing up as a Catholic, I knew St. Francis as the patron saint of animals, but the monks were new to me. They were doing their own healing on Ally, accompanied by St. Francis and the spiritual veterinarians. Part of the monks' mission was to impress on the technicians and the veterinarians in the physical world to do what is right for the animals, in addition to performing their own Divine healing on Ally and those in the hospital at the time. Armed with this new information, I knew Ally was in the best hands.

I repeated that Statement of Freedom to Ally then and every night for four nights in a row. Ally fought through every night. I also recommended that Robin tell Ally the same thing. I wanted Ally to make her own decisions. (Again, this Statement of Freedom also works on humans.) Sometimes we can hold our pets and human loved ones here on Earth for longer than is in their higher interests. They pick up on our grief or our fear of being without them. One of the most selfless things we can do for our loved ones is support them in their decision to transition when they are ready rather than when we are ready.

Early on Monday morning, Dr. Todd Bowdre telephoned to inform me he was worried about Ally. She was not progressing as well as they would have liked. She was still not eating, was lethargic, and x-rays had showed she still had a nasty infection in her lungs. I went into meditation and spoke to Ally. I asked her how she was feeling, and she kept telling me, "It hurts to breathe. My chest hurts." It also felt like Ally was overmedicated.

Dr. Bowdre mentioned that when Ally was taken outside to go potty, she walked up to all the cars in the parking lot as if she was looking for us to take her home. This thought almost broke my heart. She had been through so much, the last thing I wanted her to think was that we had abandoned her.

Armed with this new information, it was time to go to see her. I offer this suggestion to any of you that may have to endure your beloved pet undergoing any type of surgery. As evolved as Ally is, and as connected she is to me, she still felt abandoned. She knew on a soul level that was not true, but on a physical level she wasn't sure. She just needed a little reassurance from me.

Thankfully, Robin's schedule was clear for two days of that week, so I packed up some of Ally's favorite treats (sliced fresh carrots) as well as her blanket and we headed down to the vet's office. When we arrived, the receptionist escorted us to an exam room to wait for Ally and the doctor.

Dr. Osmond was on vacation at this time and Dr. Bowdre wasn't there; surgeon Dr. Kevin Bissonnette said he was not surprised Ally's recovery was taking this long, and she was progressing as well as he had expected. After all, Ally had just had her chest cracked open, part of a lung removed, and she was almost fourteen years old. Dr. Bissonnette mentioned they had removed the drainage tube on Sunday night. The biggest issue now was that Ally was not eating. They had tried everything, but she wouldn't take it. Until Ally began to eat on her own, they could not take her off the IVs. They were the only way to give Ally her pain medications and antibiotics.

It had always been Ally's nature; when she wasn't feeling good, she would stop eating. I wasn't too worried as this was her normal response. After our visit with Dr. Bissonnette, the vet technician brought Ally into the examination room. She was wrapped up in a blanket and placed on the floor. She had a sock type gauze bandage around her middle, which looked like a body suit, protecting her incision. She was out of it; she looked right through us, not seeing us at all. At first, she had no idea Robin or I were even in the room with her. I know there is a fine line between keeping the animals comfortable and overmedicating them, but I could not believe what I was seeing. Please don't get me wrong, I never want to see any animal suffering or in pain, much less one that is such a big part of my life. As I had picked up on earlier in the day, she was definitely overmedicated. But she was definitely not in any pain! Ally has always been very sensitive to medication. A little bit of pain medication goes a long way towards her pain. Just as the same discrepancies can be found in humans.

Robin and I both got down on the floor next to her, to pet her and be with her. Ally's breathing was labored, and all she wanted to do was sleep. When not with us in the exam room, she was still being housed in an oxygen crate, receiving breathing treatments, and her medication was being fed through several IV ports in her legs.

Toward the end of our visit, Ally was a little more coherent. The fentanyl had worn off slightly, and she was more like her usual self. Ally looked up at me and said, "Mary Carol, is that really you? Are you really here? I see three of you, Mary Carol." Then she looked at Robin and asked the same thing. "Robin, is that really you?" We both reassured her that we were truly there with her. She then asked me, "Am I being punished?" I immediately said, "No!" I asked her why she thought that. She replied, "I did what was asked of me, I had the surgery, and now I'm not going home. Am I being punished because I am left here?"

Ally had heard every word I was telling her on a soul level. She remembered the conversation we had about her surgery. I did my best to explain that she still needed to stay for a few nights so she could heal. While we were visiting, neither Robin or myself could get Ally to take her food or any of her treats. She just wanted to sleep. She lay down on the blanket on the floor and drifted off to sleep.

After we had been with Ally for a while, Dr. Tara Hardy and Dr. Bissonnette both came into the examination room. Dr. Bissonnette indicated Ally now had pneumonia. He asked how she had tolerated medications in the past, and what type of medication she had taken. I quickly explained her medication history, and that I truly thought Ally was overmedicated.

I was not sure if Dr. Bissonnette or Dr.

Hardy believed me when I informed them what Ally had told me earlier in the day, that her chest hurt to breathe. This was the first time Dr. Bissonnette had seen Ally. If Dr. Bissonnette didn't believe me, he should win an Oscar for his performance.

For all of you fellow fur parents reading this book, remember that you are the voice for your pets. Even the smallest detail will help the veterinarian to diagnose and heal your fur baby. When you take your pet to an emergency clinic, it might be the first time that particular vet has seen your pet. You know when your animal is not acting normal or not quite themselves. Unfortunately, our little fur babies cannot always tell us what is wrong with them. They are not like humans, who can tell you that they do not feel good.

The night vet, Dr. Bowdre, had been extremely concerned because Ally had not eaten anything immediately after her surgery. Dobermans and retrievers who have this type of surgery awake from the surgery starving. Ally did not, but that was her normal; they just didn't know that. When Ally was taking pain medications she did not have an appetite. Ironically, we tried to reassure the doctor that her behavior was actually a normal sign to us even if it wasn't a good health sign.

That works for a day or maybe two, but it had been several days now. Both Dr. Bowdre and Dr. Bissonnette decided it was a good idea to add an appetite stimulate to her medication regiment. It was vital to Ally's recovery that she would eat on her own for two reasons. One the nourishment the food would give her little body to heal. Secondly, in her food or even treats was the best way to get her to take her medications and the only way she could return home.

The problem then became, we still had to get the appetite stimulate in her little body. They usual way of forcing the pill down their throat, holding their mouth shut, blow on their nose to get then to swallow was not an option due to Ally's type of lung surgery. Personally, I don't like this method, at all.

What could I do to get her to eat? So I did what I always do. I went back into my meditation and asked God, "Now what? I've put this little dog through so much, and she isn't eating now. She isn't giving up, so how can I give up on her? What can I do?" I heard, "Talk to her. Tell her she needs to eat."

So that is exactly what I did. I visualized her in front of me, me petting her like usual, and I told her, "Ally, you have to eat to get better. You won't be able to come home until you start eating. I'm going to bring you some chicken today so you can have something different to eat."

I headed to the grocery store for a rotisserie chicken. Rotisserie chicken was always a treat for both Ally and Kody. It was a great way to get them to take their pills, too. I deboned and cut up the rotisserie chicken with my fingers. It was still warm in the container when Robin and I returned to the animal hospital for our second visit of the day.

After we arrived, we were taken to an exam room where they would bring Ally to us again. We waited for what seemed like an eternity! While we were waiting, a parade of dogs in spirit came to see us. They told us they were here to visit with Ally, to keep her calm and let her know she was loved. Among the parading ghosts of Angel puppies were several of my beloved childhood pets and Robin's first Eskie, Tall-e-ho.

That turned out to be a visit for Robin as well as for Ally. Tall-e said to Robin, "I was ready to go. I didn't want to stay any more. I don't blame you. I was in a lot of pain. I love you!" Tall-e added, "Ally isn't ready to be here yet. She needs to stay." It was a pretty lengthy conversation, and since I was playing interpreter for Tall-e, I don't remember the entire conversation.

Finally, Dr. Bissonnette appeared. He told us Ally had been off her fentanyl IV too long this morning while she visited with us, and he didn't want to disturb her this afternoon. She was resting comfortably and still in her oxygen crate. They had also started medicated breathing treatments to assist her breathing. I didn't like it, but I understood. I handed him the chicken for Ally. Robin and I left and made the two-mile drive home.

By this time, we thought Ally would be at home with us. We had been told she would be able to return to us a day after surgery, if there weren't any complications. Clearly, there had been complications. It was now day three after surgery and no Ally. Not only that, but we still had no idea when she would be able to come home. There seemed to be an improvement, but not enough to release her to come home or remove the IV ports from her limbs. We questioned ourselves — had we made the wrong decision to allow Ally's surgery and put her through this pain and suffering?

In my mind, I had supported Ally in her decision to stay on this side. She was not ready to transition. Or as Ally put it, "I'm not ready to become a real Angel puppy!" And most importantly, Ally was going to pull through this, and I would bring her home.

As we pulled into the driveway, my phone rang with Carlsbad's Veterinary Clinic number on the screen. Dr. Hardy was calling me to tell me that the minute she opened the container of chicken in front of Ally and placed it in her crate, she ate all of it. Dr. Hardy said, "She ate it as if she knew it was coming, and she was waiting for it." She did know it was coming, I told her I was bringing it to her. Ally was finally eating! One big hurdle down and closer to having her home.

After yet another day without Ally, Kody was beginning to show signs of depression and anxiety and demanded more attention from both of us. This was day five without Ally. She was still in her oxygen crate, and had developed a fever that concerned the vets. The clinic had chicken and they tried to feed it to her that night, but she would not touch it. I continued to bring her rotisserie chicken every day so Ally would eat.

Our Tuesday afternoon visit with Ally had her walking around the examination room, displaying more life than we had seen in days. She was pacing at the door, and kept saying, "Let's go! I'm ready to go home." With any excitement or exercise, Ally's breathing would become hard and labored, and her stomach experience heavy spasms. This was a new problem. It was also one of the reasons why she was still in the oxygen crate with medicated breathing treatments. Before we left, I told her she had to spend one more night in the hospital and then she could come home. All she had to do was last one more night away, and then it would be over.

She seemed to settle down a little with that information. She was being given something for her anxiety, since Dr. Bissonnette said she was very unsettled, and displayed a lot of anxiety so they were trying to calm her down. This was also a slight reaction to the Gabapentin.

    Wednesday was day six in the hospital, and on this day we were told we would finally be allowed to bring Ally home. However, an early morning call from Dr. Hardy indicated Ally's breathing was still a major concern. It hadn't improved, she continued having breathing spasms. They wanted to keep her in for a couple more days to see if the antibiotics would take effect. More x-rays indicated Ally was still suffering with a nasty lung infection plus pneumonia. Her little body was fighting as hard as it possibly could. Both Dr. Hardy and Dr. Osmond commented we had come this far, and another day or two was not going to make much difference, but it might help speed up her recovery process. Both vets recommended Ally stay for a few more nights in the hospital.

Robin and I went to visit that evening. The techs would not remove Ally from her oxygen crate as they had done in our previous visits. The vet did not want Ally to pull her away from her oxygen or her breathing treatments. So, we went to her in her crate, with clear plastic at the front. When she saw us, she recognized us immediately. I got down on the floor, opened the plastic doors, and I started to pet her. That's when her spasm breathing started again, which was frightening to see. She asked me, "Mary Carol, are we going home now? You told me one more night, and now it's time to go home." How would I tell this little dog that she was not coming home with us? I carefully told her she had to stay another night. Her breathing was out of control because she was so excited at the prospect of coming home with us. I knew we needed to leave and let her relax. It was incredibly sad to get up from the floor, and walk away, leaving Ally there for another night.

That evening I started questioning things. I knew the vets had done an incredible job in saving Ally's life. If she had been at home by herself that Thursday, she would have died a slow and painful death. If the fluid around her lungs had not been detected she would have had the back surgery and still died from the lung issues. Ally was not ready to depart this lifetime; she was fighting. She wanted to stay on the planet and come home. I struggled with the decision of whether to bring her home into a loving and healing environment or keep her at the hospital. I knew Ally was receiving amazing healing from those in spirit, and from myself. I decided to sleep on it.

On Thursday morning, which was day seven in the hospital for Ally, Dr. Boyle, who was Ally's initial intake veterinarian, called to inform me that Ally was still having difficulty breathing. She was no longer oxygen dependent, but her spasm breathing would return with activity. They had taken her off the oxygen crate, but they wanted to keep her in another night to make sure she was all right. I took a deep breath and said, "I really appreciate all you've done for Ally. However, I'm coming to get her today, and bringing her home. I can't come and visit with her today and tell her she needs to stay another night. I think it's time for me to take over her healing. I'm home with her twenty-four hours a day, she will be under my supervision. She needs the love and attention she'll get at home, which she hasn't gotten from me over the past week." Dr. Boyle and I agreed Ally would stay until later in the afternoon and then I was bringing her home.

Robin and I went to pick up Ally late afternoon on Thursday. I was handed a bag of pills, an unopened can of dog food, and three pages of "Discharge Instructions."

Ally's Case Summary from her Discharge Instructions reads as follows:

> *Ally was presented to California Veterinary Specialists surgery service for evaluation of back pain following MRI with our ER service. Upon evaluation, her respiratory rate and effort were elevated and abnormal. Radiographs and CT imaging revealed a pyothorax with consolidation of the left cranial lung lobe. Ally was taken to surgery for a median sternotomy with a left*

cranial lung lobectomy. Surgery was challenging, but overall went extremely well. Ally has shown improvement to her breathing each day while in hospital; however, she remains easily stressed with little reserves. Ally's back pain has decreased and she has continued to walk well with no neurologic deficits.

Once we received all of the "go home" instructtions, I once again scooped her up in her little pink bed and held her in my arms throughout the ride home. She was still heavily medicated.

She kept asking in the car, "Am I really going home? I thought you were going to leave me there. I thought you forgot about me. Am I really going home?"

CHAPTER 4.
ALLY'S HOMECOMING AND RECOVERY

When we arrived home, Kody was so excited to see her. He ran up to her, and started barking at all of us. Ally lifted her head from my arms and gave a low growl at him. I guess she was happy to see him, too. I carried Ally to her other bed and transferred her so she could sleep, which she did most of the evening. We were told to limit her activity, so we carried her outside to go to the potty and up and down the stairs to sleep. She primarily stayed in her bed, even to eat and drink. That evening she managed to eat her chicken and keep all of her pills down. On that first night, she slept for more than twelve hours. She would wake up in the morning in the same position in which she fell asleep. Ally was exhausted from her surgical ordeal. I think it's safe to say she was happy to be home.

Part of Ally's recovery involved restricting activity and being confined to a small room or a crate in the house. Activity of any kind could adversely affect healing and lead to an increase in complications. Even so, on day two of being home, Ally was still experiencing labored breathing. If she did any activity at all, her breathing turned into panting. Her panting moved into her hard spasm breathing. On that Friday afternoon, I checked Ally's incision to see how it was healing. When I lifted her sock bandage, I noticed it was leaving grooves in her skin. It was too tight around her front legs, rubbing her skin red. At that point, I decided to take the bandage off. The minute I removed the gauze bandage Ally's breathing improved.

By the evening, she seemed more alert. I think she realized she was home for good and finally relaxed. I could definitely see a huge improvement in her alertness and breathing. My doubts about bringing her home completely dissipated. Home was the best place for Ally to continue her healing.

As a few more days passed, Ally continued to sleep most of the time. I think she slept for four days straight, waking only for food and to go potty. She would sleep for ten hours every night, get up, go potty, and then continue to sleep in her little pink bed for another twelve hours. We kept her barricaded in the kitchen area to continue to restrict her activity. I did my best to find the perfect balance of all of her pain and anxiety meds.

Thank goodness for the pendulum, which was instrumental in measuring Ally's pain medications. (A pendulum is a device that measures energy; I have found it to be extremely beneficial for deciding on medications with pets, and also making the decision to go to the vet. You ask a yes or no question and receive an accurate answer. It is just another ancient divining tool available to all of us.)

I didn't want her to be in pain, but I knew she was still overmedicated. It seemed every time the clock struck the hour Ally needed to be given some type of pill. She was on medication for anxiety, pain, inflammation, appetite stimulant, and two different types of antibiotics for infection and pneumonia.

By day five, Ally was tired of being confined, handled, carried up and down the stairs to be taken outside. When we bent down to pick her up, she would run away from us. She did not want any help. Keeping her confined was becoming more difficult. Once we lifted the barrier and allowed her access to the den as well as the living room, she walked to every corner and to every door, like she was seeing it all for the first time, and she couldn't believe she was home.

After she had been home a week, and two weeks after her surgery, Kody developed an eye infection. His eye was red, swollen, and draining. Since Ally was due for her post-surgery check-up, Robin and I took both dogs to the vet at the same time.

When we returned to Carlsbad Veterinary Clinic I did my best to keep Ally calm before we went into the exam room. Kody has always been the friendlier of the two puppies, and able to handle other dogs better than Ally. Kody sees other dogs as friends whereas Ally sees them as threats, so Kody was making new friends in the waiting room. When it came time for Kody to go with the vet technician for evaluation, he wouldn't leave. The tech had his leash, but he did not move. Once again, Ally raised her little head from her bed, looked at him, and said, "Kody, suck it up and go! I was here for a week, you can do an hour!" He was standing next to Robin. I looked over at him, and said, "It's okay, Kody, you can go with her." Kody reluctantly went with the tech. Carlsbad Veterinary Services Clinic operates under a different type of examination method than what most pet owners have experienced; the initial exam is done without the pet parent present. It might be due to the fact that they are an emergency pet hospital, so they operate as a human emergency room clinic would.

Shortly after Kody was taken for evaluation, Robin, Ally, and I were escorted to an examination room. As we waited for the surgical staff to come for Ally, we were told Kody needed some eye tests, which only resulted in an eye drop prescription. Mitch, a vet tech, came for Ally. She was also somewhat reluctant to leave Robin and me. She kept saying, "I'm not staying! I'm not staying!" Once I reassured her that she was not remaining here, but that the vet just needed to look at her incision, she seemed to settle down and go with Mitch. As Robin and I sat there waiting, I could hear Kody whining as he does sometimes when he thinks he has been forgotten or abandoned. As soon as he realized Ally was back in the hospital section near him, he quickly settled down. I managed to get the message to him, "Kody, I can hear you! You're safe!" I recited my Protection Prayer on him again. Before I said the last word of the prayer, I felt him settling down.

Ally walked back through the exam room door being led by a new veterinarian. I am not sure if either Robin or myself were ready for what came next. Dr. Greg Ogilvie is an oncologist with their Angel Care Cancer Center division. He asked us if we knew Ally's diagnosis. I was somewhat shocked by the question. I thought the diagnosis was already clear, that she had foreign matter in her lung that had been removed. End of story. The word cancer had not been mentioned in any of my conversations with the vets. I realize that sometimes cancer cells cannot be determined unless under a microscope, but this didn't feel right to me. Dr. Ogilvie continued with Ally's diagnosis of Broncho alveolar Adeno carcinoma. He spent about thirty minutes with us, explaining the next steps and the current risks.

In Dr. Ogilvie's explanation, Ally aspirated foxtail, which was able to easily lodge itself due to the lung being severely compromised by the carcinoma. Apparently, Ally's cancer was stage three, had seventy-five percent chance of recurrence in three months, and that was only if they had removed all of the cancer from her lung. If they had not, then it would continue to grow within her body and recur more quickly. We would later learn, weeks after the surgery, that the average life expectancy of a dog after this type of surgery is seven days. Honestly, the only thing I took away from that conversation was Vinorelbine, chemotherapy, and DHA.

Maybe I was wrong, but I didn't feel or think Ally had cancer. I just wanted to get out of the examination room. Maybe I was in denial, but this did not feel real to me.

It did not resonate with me, just like the first diagnosis of Ally's back being the primary source of her pain didn't feel right to me. Unfortunately, the pathology does not lie. Ally did indeed have cancer. As she did truly have cancer, I was going to take over her healing and use the same type of God healing energy that I use on my human cancer clients. There was no way I could put this little puppy through any more pain and suffering. She needed to heal from the surgery and have a wonderful life at home, however short or long that life was going to be. A happy life without any more needles, medications or surgeries.

Please don't misunderstand me. I think the Angel Care Cancer Center does amazing work, and has helped and continues to help countless animals. Veterinary medicine has come a long way since I had pets as a child. I think that you, as the pet owner, have to do what is best for your pet. If you do choose to have your pet undergo any type of surgeries or treatments, please consider the side effects. Give your pet all of the love and extra support you can muster. It's just the healing work I do every day with my human clients gives Ally a different type of healing option that most pet owners do not have.

Robin picked up Kody's leash. I carried Ally to the car. We headed home.

A few hours later, Ally started throwing up, extensively. She managed to drink a little water. That night she slept and dry heaved during the night. At around 2:30 in the morning, I got out of bed and sat next to her, rubbing her hairless pink tummy, and reciting my God Bubble Blessing over and over again, asking the spiritual monks and St. Francis to remove her pain. She finally calmed down at about 4:30 a.m.

Several hours later, Ally awoke groggy, but came downstairs to head outside to potty. I prepared Kody's breakfast, and carried it into the utility room where they both normally eat their meals. I set down Kody's bowl and when I turned around Ally was there. She had followed me, and she looked at me and said, "Where's my breakfast?" I quickly fed her, too. Ally hadn't had any medications for twenty-four hours. No pain meds, no anxiety meds, no antibiotics. I decided to see if she could hold down her breakfast before giving her any more of her medications. I continued to use my pendulum and ask if Ally could tolerate any of her medications.

As the morning progressed, Ally seemed like her usual self again. She was bouncing off the walls and kept saying, "I'm better than ever! I feel good!" All day Sunday, her breathing was normal, she was alert, and she seemed very happy. Ally ate both of her meals, and more importantly she kept them down. I believe this little dog knew what was best for her better than any of us. She was overmedicated and her little body could no longer tolerate all of her medications. Once she threw up everything, she felt better.

Ally has not required any pain pills for her neck, chest, or back since that day we brought her home after the cancer diagnosis was shared with us. She seems to be fully healed now and happy to be home.

A few days after Ally's stomach issues, I spoke to the staff at Carlsbad Veterinary Clinic. Dr. Boyle admitted to me that none of the staff had thought Ally was going to pull through the surgery or recovery. The staff was surprised with Ally's commitment and fight to stay in the physical world. As Dr. Boyle said, "Ally is a fighter. She is a tough little girl."

It has been over nine months since Ally's surgery; she is an active, alert, and a very happy puppy. Outside of the minor nail injuries that she has accidentally self-inflicted when chasing lizards in the backyard, she is a healthy puppy. She continues to name her lizards and secure the perimeter. She will tell you that she has retired from ball playing, like Tony [Romo] of the Dallas Cowboys. When you meet her, you would have no idea of the trauma this little dog has experienced. Outside of some joint supplements, she is free of any and all medications.

One of the things I noticed that was different about Ally after this ordeal, is that her temperament has become softer. She no longer barks at other dogs or when strangers come to the door. She has become a more calm and laid back puppy. When Kody occasionally knocks her out of the way for a treat she no longer reacts.

In writing this book I asked her if she wanted to have her stamp on it, with her paw. She was excited at first, until she realized what it would entail. When I tried to paint her paw for the print, she didn't want me holding her leg. She thought I was going to put another IV in her leg. I did some healing work on that trauma, and paw print is complete. That is actually her paw print in the beginning of the book.

I am sure Ally will continue to fight and remain here on Earth until her mission in this lifetime is complete. At that time, she will become an Angel puppy in Heaven helping St. Francis and all of the other puppies in spirit.

CHAPTER 5.
THE IMPORTANCE OF THE SPIRITUAL WORLD

As you have just read, Ally experienced the miracle of healing her physical body with the assistance of many spiritual helpers. Unfortunately, most of us are not truly aware of the spiritual world, even though it can be found all around us. We move through our lives with a brief thought about God, maybe on the weekend when we go to worship. Maybe when we lose a loved one or experience a cancer scare, we quickly turn to God to forge some type of bargain or deal. God is the most important part and head of the spiritual world; the spiritual realm is multidimensional.

The human world and the spiritual world live in harmony, simultaneously. Those in spirit have a higher frequency than those in a physical body, just as several radio and tv stations can operate simultaneously but on different channels. You have read about the healing order of monks, St. Francis, and even the veterinarians in spirit that impress upon the veterinarians in the physical as to how to best heal their furry patients. Both the physical and spiritual doctors were healing Ally at the same time, and in real time. As humans, we have access to the miracle of healing from our spiritual counterparts just as the animals do.

When most people think of the spirit world the first thing that comes to mind is ghosts. There are such things as ghosts, but not in the haunting harming aspect as Hollywood would lead us to believe.

The spiritual world is made up of many different types of planets and solar systems, some known and some unknown. There are five primary planets that are the most known to us. The most well-known, and the place that we all strive to get to, is what we call Heaven. Unfortunately, there are no streets paved with gold, or St. Peter waiting at the pearly gates to allow us entry. But there is a beautiful sense of peace and overwhelming love for all its residents.

Heaven has different levels associated with it. Each level of entrance is determined by the soul's level of understanding of the love of God and His universe. The best description I received is to compare it to our education system. Those on the lower plane of spirituality, or the moral plane, would be in kindergarten. As they grow spiritually they advance in grade up to numerous advanced degrees, until we ultimately reach the level of a Master Teacher.

Hell would be what we refer to as the dark planet. This planet is where most of the not-so-nice souls live out millions of years trying to improve themselves. (Think German dictators and Russian oligarchs, and egregious offenders of mankind as occupants of the dark planet.) There is no leaving the dark planet to visit other planets. After souls on the dark planet progress and improve, they can be promoted to the gray planet. The progression requires millions of years and a tremendous amount of hard work for each soul to be elevated to the gray planet.

The gray planet is frequently referred to

in Catholic and some Christian teachings as purgatory. The souls' punishment was not as severe as to be forced to the dark planet, but with more hope to the gray planet. Once on the gray planet, the next step would be to the moral plane and then to reincarnation.

Trapped souls are in their own type of personal hell. They are souls who have died and do not realize they are dead or refuse to move on to the other side. For instance, the television series *Ghost Whisper* brought to light the trapped souls of the earth. A lot of what was depicted in the series was truthful. A trapped soul is someone who hasn't gone into slumber or started the process to the spiritual world. The soul does not realize they are dead. They refuse to move on to the spiritual world for one reason or another. They stay "haunting the earth" until their emotional issues have been resolved.

The fifth spiritual location is the Animal Planet, which we were explore in a later chapter.

All souls, trapped or otherwise, have the ability to walk among us, with the exception of those from the dark and gray planets. They are not allowed to leave until they have evolved to the point of being promoted to their next step. There is no revolving door on those planets as there is in the spiritual world, called Heaven.

Our deceased loved ones are all alive and well in one of those four places. Picture an entire universe where thoughts are things. You can create what you want by thinking it. You travel from one place to another simply by thought. Every book, class, artifact, library, and museum is there for your perusal and enjoyment.

Our spiritual helpers are all around us, whether we can see, feel, and hear them or not. They are there. We just need to listen to them. Listen with our heads, hearts and mind. We are all assigned a band of guides to assist us in our daily lives. Some of them are assigned to us at birth, others may be universal souls and have many charges and others we may pick up along the way. Before we reincarnate, we get to decide which guides or spiritual coaches are part of our spiritual group or band. The comment, "it takes a village to raise a child," is very true. It also takes a village of spiritual helpers. The most well-known members of our spiritual team are:

(1) Main Joy Guide
(2) Master Teacher
(3) Native American Indian Guide
(4) Medical Doctor
(5) Business Manager/Ph.D. Doctor

Main Joy Guide

He or she is basically the manager of our many guides and spiritual helpers, primarily in charge. For the purposes of this book, I am going to refer to the main joy guide as a female because mine is a little girl.

She has the overall day-to-day responsibilities for each of her charges. She is the first one to acknowledge or be notified of her charge needing help. When additional spiritual coaches are needed, she is also responsible for seeking out the higher or specialty guides or coaches and bringing them to help. We can have many other joy guides that support our main joy guide. Most joy guides usually appear as children, but they are tremendously old souls. Appearing as children helps them be able to get into people's hearts in the same way a young child or baby has the ability to melt a heart of an adult. Part of the main joy guide's job is to bring "joy" to our lives. The main joy guide has only one charge: you! You may have had a past life with your main joy guide, where you were both in a physical body at the same time.

Master Teacher

The Master Teacher position is usually held by someone who has elevated their spiritual understanding and subsequent spiritual growth to an unprecedented level. Being able to materialize and dematerialize in the physical world is part of the requirements of standards for a Master Teacher. The number of potential Master Teachers are countless, and come from every ethnicity, religion, and period of time.

There are an enormous number of Eastern theologically-based masters available to us in the spiritual realm. For instance, Guatama Buddha would be a more well-known

Eastern Master Teacher. Some of the Apostles and the more frequently mentioned figures in the Bible, in both the Old and New Testaments, have reached this level of mastership, such as: Moses, Jeremiah, King David, Abraham, and Samuel; the most well-known would be Jesus.

The Masters come from different types of backgrounds and organized religious affiliations, but the one thing they all have in common is they believe in God. Further, they believe that thoughts are things and what you think so you become. They have a full and true understanding and belief in God and His universe He has divinely created.

Most Master Teachers are universal souls, meaning they are there for everyone in addition to those to whom they are assigned, i.e. their charges. They are assigned to teach and assist the masses of souls trying to grow spiritually.

Native American Indian

Since the Indians are closest to the earth, they come to help us with our traveling tasks. When you first get in your car, they are present to make sure you travel safely. This encompasses all types of travel: plane, train, and anything on wheels.

They are also with us for physical protection. They can assist us with difficult physical tasks, such as when you have to lift a box that is heavy or even open a tight lid jar. Some of the most notable chiefs, braves, and squaws in our history have been assigned to guide and protect us. One of their favorite lines is, "May the Great White Spirit bless you."

Medical Doctor

Our Medical Doctor in spirit is assigned to watch over our physical body. Those gentle nudges to take it easy or to stay away from fatty comfort foods are from our Medical Doctor. When you get the feeling that something may not be right within your body, that is your spiritual Medical Doctor speaking to you. Most of our guides in this category have had past lives as being a practicing doctor of many different types in the physical. They are very familiar with the human physical body.

Business Manager/Doctor

The Business Manager/Doctor teacher is assigned to help us with our finances. Think of a business and financial advisor in the physical world. They are with us to assist in our decisions surrounding anything regarding money, purchases, and even our careers. Most of those who fall into this category have had higher education while they were on the physical plane. People who were wizards with money, business and profitable investments while they were on the physical plane are sent to help us with our finances and business decisions after they move on to the spiritual realm. Those who held doctorate degrees in finance and/or business while in the physical may also be in this category. Those spirits that were good with money while they were on earth are good examples of this category. The members of the Mayer Amschel Rothschild family are good examples of Business Manager Teachers.

Usually, you have had a past relationship with most of the members of your spiritual band. Somewhere in your past, you have a familiarity with that particular soul. He or she knows you and you know him or her. Some of us will never realize or meet our entire band of guides while we are in our physical body, but we will know someone is helping or guiding us.

A good example of spirit guides working for us in our life is the way the movie *Lifted* portrayed the spirits of deceased members in the film written and directed by Lexi Alexander. The movie portrays a father who died in Afghanistan and his spirit returns home to help his son win a singing contest. I am not sure of Lexi's background, but she definitely got a lot of this movie right. This is how our guides help us in our everyday life. Though most of us are unable to see them, some of you can probably feel them — when an idea popped into your head from somewhere, that little feeling deep in the bottom of your gut telling you something is not right, or that little voice in your head that reminds you of something. That was most probably a member of your spiritual team speaking to you. Congratulations for listening and hearing them.

The most famous or well-known of our guides in the spiritual world would be Angels. In addition to being part of the spiritual world, Angels are Universal souls and are like our first responders on earth. Just as our police officers and firefighters come to our rescue when we are in trouble or in crises, Angels are the first on the job. There are Arch Angels, who are like Master Angels in the entire angelic army. When I was a child, playing in a dirt tunnel next to a pond, the walls collapsed on me. I was buried in the earth with eight feet of dirt on top of me. There weren't any adults around, just my younger sister and a cousin. I remember screaming out for someone to help me. Then everything went dark for a moment.

Following the quick moment of darkness was this overwhelming sense of peace and light. I remember talking to this elderly man with a long white beard. In my eight-year-old Catholic brain, it was God; I would later learn it was one of my Master Teachers, Moses. To me it seemed like a long enjoyable conversation. It felt to me as if time stood still. He told me that it was my decision if I went back or not. He continued to tell me that I would have a tremendous amount of work to do in this lifetime. I was told that I could choose to stay with him and learn or return to my life and fulfill my work. I looked down and watched my sister and my cousin frantically digging in the dirt at the base of the tunnel.

The next thing I remember I was raising my right arm up through the dirt. I was at the surface, no longer eight feet under the earth. I brushed the dirt from my face and yelled to my family. My cousin asked me how did I get up there? "You were down here. What happened?" I didn't have an explanation for her. I wasn't sure what to tell her. I didn't think anyone would believe me. I wasn't sure I believed it all myself.

Later, through past life regression therapy, meditation, and medium trance sessions, I learned my Joy Guide, Posey, called out to an Angel to help me. Angel Gabrielle came to my rescue that day in the tunnel. She arrived with the much-needed oxygen to keep my little body alive while I had my conversation with Moses. When she received the message that I was going to return to my body, she raised my physical body to the top of the earth that covered me; she is the one who brought my face and one arm above the surface. Only my eyes, nose, and mouth were exposed to the air; my right arm was buried, but only by a light cover of dirt. I had no injuries at the time. Later, I would develop some dental issues due to the trauma and jarring of the dirt slamming my jaws shut. I made the half-mile walk back to our camp house and never mentioned my conversation with Moses to anyone. We told no one about the other events, either.

From that day forward, my intuition, my ability to read people's and animals' energies, has only become intensified. I have known things before other people did. I have seen things before they happened. I saw people in spirit more vividly than in physical life. My dreams became more intense and more frequent. It was by no means the intensity or the level that I have today, but it was stronger. The blessing that came out of that buried-in-the-earth tragedy is that it gave me the road map to navigate between the worlds, with frequency and ease. Still I told no one. Who was going to believe me?

Years passed, relationships as well as jobs came and went. But I still had a long way to go. I had a lot of issues to work through on my own, before I could truly step into this role of a true spiritual healer and be able to help other people and animals. Healer heal thyself. Most people don't understand that if you want to help someone, you must clear your own crap first. I can tell you there was a tremendous amount of pain, trauma, and hurt that needed to be healed within myself. I needed to become a different and a better person in order to be able to grow with this healing energy. While I walked the clearing path, I made a lot of mistakes along the way, but I learned many hard-fought lessons in those steps. Lessons I can now apply to my clients and their beloved pets.

The spiritual world and all that it has to offer is here to support, protect, and assist man, in a manner quite similar to the animals. It's one more gift at the fingertips of mankind. All you have to do is to realize that it is there, access it, and utilize it much like

Dorothy in the *Wizard of Oz* — she always had the ability to go home with her ruby slippers; she just didn't know it. Glenda, the good witch, had to give Dorothy the information on how to get home.

So, my friends, consider me your spiritual Glenda!

CHAPTER 6.
WHY DID GOD PUT ANIMALS ON THE PLANET?

This is an easy question to answer. The short answer is…animals were put on Earth to support people and by extension, the planet! There are many different ways animals are on the planet to support humankind. As it has been explained to me, God created this beautiful planet Earth in perfection by His divine design. He created a safe and conducive setting for humans to heal, learn their life lessons, and to grow spiritually.

By adding animals, more specifically domestic animals, these other living beings were to show us humans how to love and how to be loved unconditionally. In fact, everything on the planet is designed to support humans and to assist them in reaching their ultimate potential. In this perfect environment, He created the optimum balance of plants and animals. In simplistic terms, plants were created as a food source and also to supply oxygen essential for the survival of man and animals. Animals serve a much larger role in our lives. Here are four of the most noted options.

Animals as Workers

Working animals have a huge diversity of performance ranging from transportation to hunting to emotional support to assisting the blind. History tells us that in 275 B.C. the Romans captured elephants to be used in war at Carthage. Five years later, King Pyrrhus of Epirus brought twenty elephants to attack the Romans at the battle of Heraclea.

Another notable working animal is the ox. These beasts of burden have been used for centuries to move plows through rough terrain to prepare fields to grow crops and as the ancient day trucks to move heavy objects. Egyptian hieroglyphs from thousands of years ago show oxen pulling plows and soldiers on horseback.

Notably, cattle have historically been used more than horses as draft animals whereas before the automobile, horses served as the primary source of transportation, from war to everyday travel. Today we still use the term horse-power as a unit of measurement. Ancient Egyptians held cats in the highest esteem; it was a crime to harm or kill a cat. They were rumored to be the guardians of the underworld.

One of my favorite workers of the animal kingdom is the little worker bee. Most people see bees simply as a nuisance. Yet these small and hardworking insects actually make it possible for many of your favorite foods to reach your table. Bees are one of a myriad of other animals (including birds, bats, beetles, and butterflies) called pollinators, which transfer pollen and seeds from one flower to another, fertilizing the plant so it can grow and produce food. Without bees to spread seeds and pollinate flowers, many plants—wild plants and food crops—would die, even becoming extinct.

Today, I believe dogs have made the biggest advancement in their support of humans. There are still working dogs on battlefields as attack dogs and to protect their handlers. In airports, train stations, and cargo containers they are taught to find explosives, drugs, and other contraband on persons and in cargo. Dogs are being trained to be medical assistants in sensing the drop-in blood sugar levels in humans, and the onset of seizures before they happen. Some are even utilized as transporters to retrieve insulin and other lifesaving medications when their human is not able.

In addition, dogs make the perfect emotional support animals for anxious and abused children. Some are being trained to not only be emotional support for veterans, but also to be a physical support for them as well as for mobility-impaired individuals.

Animals as Companions

This one, I believe, is the most important. Unlike the performance of specific tasks, an animal's value as a companion might be more difficult to measure. With human association and their domestication, animals have become objects of affection and even sometimes obsession. Florence Nightingale observed small pets helping reduce anxiety in psychiatric patients, and Sigmund Freud used his dog Jofi to help diagnose the level of tension in his patients.

Small animals are also being used to alleviate the stress and anxiety in children when they are called to testify in abuse cases. Most skilled nursing, assisted living centers, and hospitals have a day where they may provide "four-legged therapy."

There are many different types of certification programs available to animal owners that can be obtained through the assistance of trained dogs and handlers. These include cognitive and social functioning to autism, seizure detection, and emotional support. Dogs are being trained to be physical stabilizers for wounded veterans and to be hands and legs for amputees.

Research has confirmed the effectiveness of equine therapy, or hippotherapy, showing that it lowers blood pressure and heart rate, alleviates stress, and reduces symptoms of anxiety and depression. Equine therapy also helps people struggling with addictions and mental health disorders develop the following skills for healthy living.

The most important piece of animal interactions as companions is to show man how to love and be loved, unconditionally. A dog does not hold a grudge. A dog is always happy to see you, no matter how he was treated when you left. They greet you at the door, tail wagging, with unconditional love. How many humans do you know practice that kind of unconditional love?

A dog, cat, or even other animals are companions to man. I also think animals are here to help us heal our own emotional issues even before we realize we have them. Animals can be the perfect mirror of our own behavior and emotional stressors, proving to be the mirror so we can see and identify what we need to change, heal, or remove in our own lives. They can sense the needs, fear, and excitement in humans. How many times have we been told that a dog senses your fear? It's true—animals of all types can sense or pick up on a human's and other animals' emotions.

They are also here to be of service to man and to support the earth so that humans can learn and grow. Animals provide a different type of love and support to mankind that man does not receive from another human. The pure existence of animals on the planet provides an ecological paradise so that man can simply exist.

It is easy to see how a domesticated animal such as a dog or a cat can bring unconditional love to everyone. Take Ally and Kody, for instance. They are both loved very much, and they give love in return. They are capable of taking away stress and anxiety in the household. Dogs can bring a sense of calm to those around them.

There are service dogs, which perform physical duties for the injured, and emotional service or support dogs, which visit assisted living or nursing homes to bring joy to the residents. It always works for me! If I am feeling down or stressed, I grab one of the puppies and hug them.

Animals as Resources

Cattle, pigs, poultry, and fish feed us, but the consumers buying their meat as food are far removed from the animals themselves. The United Stated Department of Agriculture puts 2016 meat consumption levels of 56.5 billion pounds of beef alone. Beef exports from the United States added $6.4 billion dollars to the economy. Many families in the United States depend upon the growth and sale of animals for a source of income.

According to *And Other Furry Friends* by Michal Addady, published in *Forbes* magazine, dated August 26, 2016, the American Pet Products Association found that owners of fish, birds, dogs, cat, horses, and other reptiles are expected to spend over $62.75 billion dollars nationwide on their pets. Of the $60.28 billion, $23.05 billion was spent on food and $15.42 billion on veterinary care. Services (including grooming, boarding, training, supplies, over the counter medicine, and toys) comprise $19.69 billion of this total. The remaining $2.12 billion was spent toward live animal purchases. Sure seems to be a lot of money spent on poop bags, sparkle bows, and treats!

Animal Roles in the Ecosystem

Animals also play a crucial role in the function and development of the planet. An ecosystem is a community of animals, plants, and microbes that sustain themselves in the same area or environment by performing the activities of living, feeding, reproducing, and interacting. It is a relationship that exists between all the components of an environment. It includes plants, animals, fish, and micro-organisms, including soil, water, and people. Our ecosystem depends upon their input and survival.

Within the ecosystem, organisms are grouped into producers or consumers. Ecosystems study the flow of energy through them. Energy from the sun usually enters the ecosystem through the plants or producers. Producers convert energy from the environment into sugar or glucose.

Every little animal within the ecosystem has a vital role in the well-being of the planet. If one species is rendered extinct due to some imbalance, it can have significant cascading effects throughout the rest of the chain. For example, and returning to one of my favorite animals mentioned earlier, even a small bee is in fact a crucial worker in the factory of nature. Plants, flowers, and grasses do not bloom without their pollen-carrying role. Even man's ability to grow certain crops is affected by the presence or absence of bees in certain cases. When the numbers of bees become low, people rent hive units and install them on properties to encourage colonization and thus pollination.

Another important part of the chain is predators. Carnivores are usually seen as a threat and usually hunted for safety or even sport. However, we notice that when their numbers are reduced, the populations of deer, rabbits, and other fast-reproducing species quickly become too large in numbers, causing problems. Predators are important to the ecosystem since they help in keeping other animal populations in check. Some animals work in balance with one another in the quest for survival. When one of the pair is taken to extinction or their numbers get too low, the other of the pair suffers.

A final aspect of animals in the environment are scavenger animals. Coyotes play an important role in an ecosystem not only as a key predator of rodents, but also as scavengers. Scavengers, including coyotes, crows, ravens, vultures, and many other species of animals, play a major role in maintaining a healthy habitat. Many birds, rats, and even catfish are all considered scavenger animals. Scavenging is both a carnivorous and an herbivorous feeding behavior, as the scavenger feeds on both dead animal and plant material present in its habitat.

Scavengers' primary role in our ecosystem is to consume the dead animal and plant material. Dead animals are a health hazard to living animals as they can spread disease, but scavengers quickly break down the dead biomass, and everyone in the ecosystem benefits. On a very detailed note, detrivores and decomposers complete this process by consuming the remains left by scavengers. The Earth would soon be covered in dead organisms if there were not some way of removing of all the dead plants and animals. Detrivores are organisms that obtain nutrients by feeding on large parts of decaying animals and plants, and also on waste material. Earthworms, many types of beetles, and some sea birds are detrivores.

The Balancing Act

Each animal plays a role to help keep the balance in nature. Animals that feed primarily on plants bring about a balance in the plant world. Certain plant species that can be harmful to the growth of other organisms may be the favorite food of a particular animal; if the plant is left to grow unchecked, it could spread, and this could bring about a damage to the ecosystem.

I think the best of example of an ecosystem being out of balance would be the Florida Everglades. The Everglades hosts 1,301 species of native flora that are tropical or subtropical in nature, which arrived on the Florida peninsula about 5,000 years ago. Winds, water, and birds carried most of the tropical flora. The subtropical species spread from more northern locations. As of 2010, 1,392 additional non-native plant species have been identified and established themselves in South Florida.

Yet it has some problems with its special nature (no pun intended). A variety of avenues are available for species to be brought by humans deliberately or by accident: agricultural experiments, shipping containers, or attached to vehicles. South Florida is a transportation hub for shipping and traffic between the U.S. and the Caribbean and Central and South America. In 1990, 333 million plants were brought into Miami International Airport.

More than fifty species of exotic mammals have been recorded in South Florida, at least nineteen of which are self-sustaining. Colonies of feral mammals are established in or around the Everglades including dogs, pigs, and cats. Wild animals native to other parts of the U.S. have also been established, including nine-banded armadillos and coyotes.

Florida has enacted laws to prohibit the release of exotic animals into the wild. To dissuade people from dumping animals, local authorities have begun holding "Non-native Amnesty Days" in several Florida locations where pet owners who are no longer willing or able to take care of non-traditional pets such as snakes, lizards, amphibians, birds, and mammals—excluding dogs, cats, and ferrets—can deposit animals without being prosecuted for illegal dumping of exotic species. The state of Florida has also held its Python Challenge, which attracts hunters from all over the United States to legally hunt the snakes in order to lessen the snake population of the Everglades.

I think that I was one of the lucky ones, growing up in a home that was filled with many different types of animals, which created and fostered an empathy for all of our furry, finned, and feathery friends. As a child, my brother, sister, and I had many different dogs, cats, fish, and even rabbits as pets. We were famous for taking in strays of all kinds. Then there were the unwanted animals that were close by as well: the rats, mice, snakes, armadillos, Texas horny toads, bullfrogs, and buzzards.

Part of my daddy's profession was raising cattle on his many pastures in Texas. There was one little calf in particular that was closer to my heart than the others. She was a Hereford breed, my daddy's bovine breed of choice. Herefords have a signature rust red brown body with a white face and legs. Her mom had over indulged in the fresh green clover grass in the pasture shortly before giving birth. When this happens, it can cause the animal to die of bloat (a digestive disorder characterized by an accumulation of gas in the first two compartments of a bovine's stomach).

Unfortunately, her mom didn't make it. My daddy brought the calf home to me to feed and care for. If it happened to be a Saturday morning and I wanted to sleep in, she would let me know she was hungry by going to my bedroom window and letting out a loud bellow until I came out with a fresh bottle of powdered milk. If I was late for her afternoon feeding, she would walk onto the porch, bellow loudly, and slobber all over the sliding glass door. I named the calf Clover, and she lived in our backyard for over a year before daddy put her with the herd in the pasture near the house. After the integration, I would go out to the pasture and yell her name and she would come running. Many years later, she would still come to me if I called her.

You learned that I have a history with all

types of animals! I grew up with them; I have raised them and loved them. But what about those animals that never see or come into contact with humans? Outside of keeping the food chain supported, those "wild" animals continue to give loving energy into the ground, which is transference of their positive energy then distributed to every part of the Earth. It energizes the food we grow and eat, the trees, grass, plants in the ground, and finally into the humans inhabiting the planet.

Grass, trees, and all of the plant species have a positive energy and a purpose on the Earth just as animals do. While walking on grass or being surrounded by beautiful plants and trees, we absorb that wonderful energy through our bare feet and even our arms. The same premise can be applied to all foliage and the plant kingdom. Both the plant and animal kingdoms are vitally important to the survival of mankind.

The Real Animal Planet

All animals have souls. Their spiritual composition is identical to a human's. When they die, their souls leave their bodies in the same way human souls leave the human body. The only difference is that an animal can only show love; they do not create karma or karmic debts. If an animal bites or is aggressive, there is a human behind that negative behavior because that is not the nature of the animal. Make no mistake, if a human was unkind to an animal, that human will have created his or her own bad karma. That karma is something for which the human will have to atone and make restitution on some level to the animal.

Though animals reincarnate in the same way as humans do, but they do not have as much preparation as a human soul when they pass from a physical to spiritual plane. If you have a pet that you were instantly attracted to, that animal was probably yours in a previous lifetime. Your pets will seek you out in future lifetimes. Animals do not transmigrate (i.e., a human does not reincarnate as a dog in one lifetime and a human in another), and neither do humans, which means the link of the relationship remains constant between lifetimes of humans and their companion animals.

Within the dog family (or any animal family), an animal can change the type or the breed it wishes to be, but not transmute to a different animal. For example, a little calico kitten could have been a huge lion, king of the jungle, in its previous life incarnation, or a standard collie could have been a teacup poodle. However, a bulldog could not have been a tiger. The soul of every animal that was ever created is alive and existing on the Animal Planet.

Through my spiritual studies of past lives, I learned that Ally was mine in several past life-times. In one lifetime, Robin and I were sisters, living in Rhode Island in the late 1800s. Ally was our little dog. We would dress her up in doll and baby clothes and take her for walks in a little pink stroller. She had a matching little pink doll bed in our room. I think we carried her everywhere. She was a true little princess. To this day her favorite color is pink sparkle. I know dogs are color blind, but Ally will always choose pink. It might be the energy it projects.

Animals have a special heaven, or animal

spiritual planet, to go when they shed their physical bodies and transition to the other side. They are allowed to visit the human spiritual Heaven, if they would like to see their departed loved ones. Animals in spirit are allowed to travel to the other parts of the spiritual world. They are allowed to visit their past owners in spirit and in the physical, if they chose to do so.

Their time in between incarnations is considerably shorter than a human. They can have several lifetimes with the same owner if they so wish to do so. Also, animals do not have lessons to learn, as humans do. They do not have karmic debts to repay or grudges. If they were abused or neglected by a previous owner, they will come in with that victim energy, characteristics, and behavior. They are pure love with a purpose on the planet.

In my opinion, I think God put dogs on the planet and in our individual lives to teach humans several extremely essential life lessons. Humans have a tendency to get caught up in being right and holding onto anger, bitterness, and resentment in their lives. Resentment is like drinking poison and expecting the other person to die. It does poison us.

Dogs teach us how to love unconditionally. No matter how much trauma or abuse a dog has endured, it is always open to being loved and giving love. They are constantly open to forgiveness and rehabilitation. Just as with humans, the power of touch is essential to their bonding with humans. If humans lived their lives with these dog lessons, society would be a better place and we could indeed have peace on Earth. If you need more convincing, God spelled backward is dog.

CHAPTER 7.
HELPFUL TIPS FOR BETTER PET RELATIONSHIPS AND A HAPPIER HEALTHIER PET

On a personal level, I feel as though I need to speak for the animals. Having pets, specifically dogs, has evolved through the years; it has definitely become a different experience today than when I was growing up with pets. Below is a list of suggestions I hope will enhance your pet-to-human experience and relationship. Remember, there are not any bad dogs, just uninformed dog owners.

1. **Research the type of dog that best fits your lifestyle.** Make a list of what you are wanting in your next new pet and what activities you will be doing with it. Do you intend on traveling with your pet? Is the pet going to be left alone a lot? Even if you want

to rescue a dog from a shelter or pound, do research as to what type of breed would be best suited to you. Check for size, activity level, health issues, life expectancy, and temperament. Make sure you spend some quality time with the animal before you take your new pet home because it would not be good for you or the pet if you would have to return it after you have brought it home.

2. **Find a good veterinarian**. There are many veterinarians available to you. Some are great, and some are not so good. Take the time to interview your new veterinarian. Read the reviews online. Go to his or her office, meet the staff. Consider if the facility is clean and pet friendly. Is the front office staff friendly or angry looking? Find a veterinarian with whom you and your pet feel comfortable. Watch your pet's behavior while interacting with the vet. I always use the pendulum I mentioned earlier to check to see if a vet is good for Ally or Kody. A pendulum is a device that measures energy; I have found it to be extremely beneficial for deciding on medications with pets, and also making the decision to go to the vet. You ask

a yes or no question and receive an accurate answer. It is just another ancient divining tool available to all of us. Learning to use this tool will enhance not only your pet's life but your own.

3. Do not expose your pet to any type of second-hand smoke or other toxic chemicals. Since humans are at a higher level (literally, I'm talking about height here) than our pets, we don't always take into account what types of poisons or toxins are down low. Make sure your floor or carpet cleansers are not toxic to your pet. Make sure your yard is also free of toxic materials. Fertilizers, poisons, and even different types of mulch can be harmful to your pets. Remember if your pet walks on grass with poisonous chemicals that will also be brought into your home; your pet can lick its paws and ingest the chemicals in addition to them being absorbed through its skin. After all, it is not a good idea to have your human family exposed to any of it either.

4. Make sure to remember to keep your pets' vaccinations and preventative medica-

tions current. Beyond annual vacations, flea medications are vital to your pet's health (and also deter ticks). Outside from the obvious (that flea bites cause pain and even anemia in your pet), they also carry tapeworms. Also put your pet on a heartworm prevention. Going to the vet and getting these medications is the easy part; remembering to give them the meds is another. The medications will not work if they are sitting on the counter and have not been given to your pet.

5. Make sure your dog learns basic training commands. There are seven common commands. Brandon McMillan (host of the television show *Lucky Dog*) can help with this one. Brandon's seven common commands are: sit, stay, don't touch, come, heel, down, and off. There are many reputable and positive dog and owner trainers available. Find one both you and your dog like. A well-behaved dog is definitely easier to manage. It can only enhance your relationship.

6. Make sure you keep their teeth clean,

either professionally or on your own. Good oral hygiene is essential to a dog's overall health. In addition, invest in treats that clean their teeth and keep their breath fresh. There is even a toothbrush treat with a Cosequin supplement added to it (which is great for their joints). It offers two benefits in one treat.

7. **If your pet has to have surgery or stay in the pet hospital, visit as soon as you are allowed.** Sit with your pup, reassure him or her that he or she is going to be alright. Say you love (insert your pet's name to personalize the statement, which means even more to your dog). When it comes time to leave, please make sure your pet is picked up or taken away before you leave. The last thing you want is your dog to see you walk away and leave them there. Let the veterinarian technician take your dog away or block the dog's vision while you leave.

I must emphasize, the last thing you want your pet to see is you walking out the door and leaving them behind. That can be devastating to your animal. As evolved as Ally is and as connected she is to me, she still felt abandoned when I left the exam room that first time. She knew on a soul level it was not true, but on a physical level she wasn't sure. Ally was like any pet undergoing surgery, who needs that physical reassurance that he or she hasn't been abandoned and are still loved. The best way to alleviate any abandonment issues is to physically touch them, be there with them even if only for a few minutes. If I had to do this all over again, I would go down there the afternoon after Ally's surgery. I would be there when she first opened her little eyes.

8. During a veterinarian visit, put one hundred percent focus on your pet. Before a visit to the vet's office, or even the groomers, take your dog for a walk (if they are able, of course). This exertion of energy and happy time with you will help them feel more relaxed and calm. Remember your animal is going to pick up on your energy and your mood. Make sure you are remaining calm to, from, and during your vet appointment. If you are calm, they will be calm. If your pet likes to be held, hold them. Pet them while you are waiting in the lobby and in the exam room. Even get down on their level, be it the floor or the chair next to them, in order to pay attention to them. Put your phone away and be present with your pet. It will make a difference by transforming what otherwise could be a horrible experience from your pet's perspective into a more pleasant one.

9. Be ready to get down and dirty. With Ally and Kody, I wear clothes I can get dirty when we go to the vet or even the groomers. If they are both nervous, I get down on the floor with them to hug them, pet them, tell them it's alright, and that they are safe. They respond by being calm and happy.

10. Document their behaviors prior to going to the vet's office. Before you go to the vet with an ache or behavior issue, it is always a good idea to document the behavior or physical conditions. With cell phones these days, it is easy to take photo or a video. That will help the vet with the diagnosis. Pay attention to what is normal and what is not. The more you notice what is out of the ordinary, the easier it will be for the vet to diagnose your pet's conditions. Remember you are the voice of your pet.

11. Help your pet take medications. Some dogs will take their pills with no issues. Hiding them in their favorite treat or in store bought pill pockets will work. You can also try a hot dog, peanut butter, cream cheese, chicken, turkey, or cheese. It could be included in their usual dog food. Sometimes the more creative you become, the easier it is to get them to take their pills. But if you have a puppy like Ally who has taken her fair share of pills in her lifetime, it can become rather difficult. In the past I could hide her pills in rotisserie chicken. Lately that hasn't been working. I had to get creative.

After exhausting the above options, I sought out new ones. What I ended up doing was to purchase the empty gelatin capsules, cut the pills into small enough pieces to fit in the capsules and hide them in her food. Since the full capsule was too large for her, I used each half, with a small piece of the pill, left one end open. I trimmed the capsule to match the small pill. I shoved the open-end capsule into her dog food, and mix it with the rest of her food then add some pieces of turkey lunch meat. This combination works today, but keep in mind your dog's requirements might change. What works today might not work tomorrow.

12. Never raise your voice to your pet. I know it's sometimes second nature to yell at your pet when they are doing something wrong. There are much better and more effective methods of discipline. One of my favorite attention-getters is an empty dry plastic water bottle filled with lose change. A combination of smaller coins like pennies, dimes, and nickels works best. Make sure you replace the cap, otherwise you might get a money shower! Shake the bottle when you need to get your pet's attention in order to stop the unwanted behavior. If you need something louder, you can use two pot lids as cymbals. Or a spoon on a pot lid. Try it lightly, not at full crash. You don't want to traumatize your pet.

13. Take your dog on short drives to acclimate him to an automobile ride and go somewhere other than the vet's office. If the only place they ever go is to the vet, they will start to have a negative memory attached to moving vehicles. But if you add in the groomer's shop, the dog park, or the beach, he won't mind the car ride as much. Acclimating slowly is your best option.

14. If you have to be gone, keep the television or radio on for your pet. Make sure the music or programs played on that station or channel are soothing, not violent. Family programming is best. Choose elevator or classical music if you use the radio rather than the television. Most family programming movies makes for a great pet sitter. Ally loves *Cinderella* and *Heartland* while Kody prefers *Snow Dogs* and *The Walton's*.

15. In the first few weeks, don't leave them alone for longer than an hour at a time. Pets need time to adjust to their new surroundings. They need to be reassured they are safe and that you will not abandon them. Remember what you do in the beginning will train them for their future. Consistency is key. Start with an hour and work up to the full time you will be gone. Add thirty minutes additional time, every other day. Reward them with a treat when you leave and also when you return. Upon your return take the time to speak to them, giving them some attention before you move about your day.

16. Make sure they have a place to call their own. Create a safety zone for them. Purchase them their own pet bed or a crate. Give them their own towel or even a blanket. Remember to keep it clean. Pet bedding, just like human bedding, needs to be cleaned. I would suggest something that doesn't have to be dry cleaned, but can be easily thrown into the washer. You might want to add an amethyst or rose quartz crystal to their bed at home. The crystal needs to be big enough so the dog cannot try to swallow it if you can't put it inside the lining. However, in my years of crystal practice with animals, I have never heard or seen an animal try to eat, chew, or swallow a crystal. They intuitively know it's there to help them. It will provide continuous healing and keep them calm. Also, unless you have two small little dogs that love to snuggle each other, don't let other dogs share their bed.

17. I recommend feeding them twice a day. I do once in the morning and once in the evening. How happy would you be if you only ate once every twenty-four hours? You might also want to leave dry pet food out when you are gone from home.

18. Make sure your pet food is of high quality and is positive food. By this I mean the food needs to have positive energy. Secondly, make sure the food is positive food for them, meaning that their bodies can tolerate the food you are giving them. Add supplements or vitamins to your pet's daily routine, such as Cosequin and DHA. The best way to test the energy level of their food is by using a pendulum. I would also test the supplements in the same way. Do the supplements have positive energy? Does the animal need the supplement? How much does the animal need? Can the animal tolerate the supplement? Don't forget to always have a large bowl of clean water available to them at all times.

19. Please do not leave your pet in the car. In December of 2016, California approved a statute that provides that *no person shall leave or confine an animal in any unattended motor vehicle under conditions that endanger the health or well-being of an animal due to heat, cold, lack of adequate ventilation, or lack of food or water, or other circumstances that could reasonably be expected to cause suffering, disability, or death to the animal. A conviction for this violation carries a fine from $100.00 to $500.00 and/or imprisonment not to exceed six months for the first violation.* If you have to leave them in the car, then it might be a good idea to leave them at home.

One of my personal pet peeves, pun intended, is to see a truck driving on the Interstate at seventy-plus miles per hour with a dog loose in the truck bed. I want to pull the truck over, put the dog in the cabin of the vehicle, yank the driver to the truck bed, and show the human how it feels. Please don't put your dog in the back of a vehicle; treat them as a member of the family. You shouldn't put your child in the back of an open vehicle so please don't do it to your pet.

20. Sometimes it is easier to have two pets instead of one. Yes, this is double the commitment and double the expense, but it's double the love! And you will have a built-in babysitter. Sometimes dogs do better with a companion. Make sure they are compatible.

21. Exercise is a form of tranquilizer. Exercise is an important factor in your pet's overall health. They need to be able to play, run, and go on walks. Exercise releases any anxiety they may have. Please do some research on how much exercise your pet's breed and age requires and follow through; it's also important when considering a new pet that you have the time and ability to meet the exercise needs. It might be a good way for you to get some exercise in, too.

22. Have your pet spayed or neutered. Unless you are a loving, qualified breeder, please have your pet fixed. Pet responsibility starts in the very beginning of pet ownership.

23. When that day arrives, there is no other choice but to let go. Your pet is in pain and there is nothing else that can be done for them. You have recited my prayer of freedom to them. Remind them you love them.

Sometimes you have told them it is alright to let go, but they haven't been able to move to the other side on their own, so you find yourself at the vet's office for assistance. Please make sure you stay with your pet through the entire process. Pet him, sit with him, remind him you will see them again— you absolutely will.

24. Remember, owning a pet is a commitment. You are taking on the well-being and responsibility of a perpetual two-year-old. Your pet will never grow up, will never feed himself or herself, never go out without you. They will always continue to rely upon you for everything. There will be vet bills. Even if you are lucky enough to have a healthy pet, there will still be checkups, vaccinations, food, treats, grooming, day care, pet sitters, and so on. Pet ownership is an emotional, time, and financial commitment. You don't want to have your pet ten years, and all of a sudden decide it's too expensive or you are not wanting to dedicate the time. Dogs crave and need their human companions' love and attention.

25. Remember to love them because they will always love you, unconditionally. Give them physical hugs. Look into their eyes and tell them that you love them every day. Pet them. I spend a few minutes every night on the floor with Ally and Kody, petting them as they stretch out for the night. I also say my God's Bubble Blessing over them. It keeps them safe, relaxes them, and heals them while they sleep. Just like any relationship, whether human to human or human to pet, you will get out of the relationship, what you put into it. Remember God spelled backward is dog. I think God put dogs on the planet to show us how to love one another. They learn to forgive and trust quickly. As humans, we need to learn that lesson.

26. Guided meditations to help your pet. There are two guided meditations on my business portal available for download for both you and your pet. One of these meditations will help you allow your fur baby the freedom to make the decision they truly desire. The other one is something you can do to keep pets calm and healthy.

ABOUT THE AUTHOR

Mary Carol Ross is a former legal corporate international road warrior. She served more than twenty-five years in the corporate world before stepping into her true calling and creating an innovative type of healing in Spiritual Archaeology. At a very young age, Mary Carol discovered she could see, feel, and read people's emotions and traumas from their past and present. She can see into a physical body and the emotional body; she views the issues, emotions, and blocks within that are in need of healing.

Mary Carol hid her true gifts behind anger, fear, and resentment, which caused her to choose the wrong path at almost every opportunity. She walked a long hard road, and experienced many difficulties in her thoughts, decisions, actions, and inactions. Mary Carol self-medicated with food, toxic relationships, and retail therapy as she attempted to make herself feel whole and loved. It was not until she realized she needed to heal the source of her pain that she finally freed herself from self-destructive habits and actions.

Mary Carol began the Spiritual Archaeology journey of exploring and healing, which helped her uncover who she truly is and who she came here to be in this lifetime. During this journey, she discovered she had a tremendous connection to the spiritual side of life along with medium abilities. A near-death experience was the catalyst to enable her to move from the Earth plane and the spiritual world with frequency and ease.

The first part of her life was full of wrong choices, hard lessons, tears, sorrow, and pain. Gradually with her spiritual work, it became a path of soul as well as personal growth, forgiveness, and acceptance. Along the way, Mary Carol perfected her techniques, uncovered many hidden talents, and developed gifts that allow her to help and heal people, animals, and the planet.

Mary Carol Ross holds certifications as a Medical Intuitive, Professional Life Coach, Career Intuitive, Hypnotist, Past Life Regression Therapist, Master Intuitive, Crystalline Healing Master, Medium, Transitional Therapist, and Mediator.

She lives in San Diego, California, where she bases her world-wide healing practice. More can be learned about her methodology through her website:

www.marycarolross.com

www.ingramcontent.com/pod-product-compliance
Lightning Source LLC
Chambersburg PA
CBHW021127300426
44113CB00006B/317